5:2
LIFESTYLE

more than 100 recipes plus
4 weeks of menu plans

DELPHINE DE MONTALIER
& CHARLOTTE DEBEUGNY

PHOTOGRAPHY BY CHARLOTTE LASCÈVE

MURDOCH BOOKS

CONTENTS

Delphine de Montalier and Charlotte Debeugny have been passionate about healthy and balanced eating for a long time. The aim of this book is to adapt the 5:2 diet to French cuisine, which has a rich gourmet heritage, by using fresh and delicious ingredients in new, creative ways.

Their unique concept is the "Super 500"

This is a dish that contains the maximum amount of vitamins and minerals while obeying the rule of only 500 or 600 calories on the two weekly Fast Days. These meals reduce the time spent in the kitchen, as you only need to cook once during the day. They can be prepared the day before and they're portable, so you can enjoy them at work or when you're on the move. Lastly, they offer the perfect balance of protein, carbohydrates, and vegetables to ensure you're full of health and vitality. With energy and a positive outlook, you'll get through the Fast Days without too much difficulty, if any!

5:2 COACHING

Can you really lose weight by dieting only two days per week?

"Intermittent fasting" is the latest trend in dieting. Originating in the United Kingdom, it has spread around the world. Based on solid research, it has been scientifically proven effective, unlike many fashionable diets.

The basic principle is to eat less, which allows you to lose weight and offers numerous health benefits.

The advantage of this method? Flexibility!

You don't need to eat less every day, only on certain days. These are the Fast Days. There should be at least two Fast Days per week. It's referred to as the 5:2 diet, because each week you have two days of restricted eating and five "normal" days, the Non-Fast Days. After a month of intermittent fasting, or only nine days of restricted caloric intake, weight loss can reach up to 7 pounds, or even more. So why not try it? Many people focus on what they should eat on the Fast Days. The advice is to eat no more than 25 percent of the usual recommended calorie intake, which comes to about 500 calories for women and 600 calories for men. But it's also important to make good choices about what you eat on the other five days.

Can you really eat absolutely anything, including hamburgers, fries, and unlimited chocolate cake?

Of course, you can have dessert and drink alcohol on the Non-Fast Days if you like. But eating like a sparrow for two days and then gorging on junk food on the other five is far from healthy, even if you obey the rules of intermittent fasting! The aim is to make balanced and tasty meals on the Non-Fast Days just as you do on the Fast Days, so you feel fit and stay that way.

Why should you eat less?

Studies on animals have shown that a reduction in calorie intake leads to weight loss, improved physical condition, and longer life expectancy. However, it can be difficult to subject yourself to a limited calorie intake on a permanent basis. This is why scientists have begun to examine the effectiveness of restricting calories on a limited number of days, allowing the animals to eat their fill on other days. This method has proved to be effective: alternating fasting days and days of "normal" eating has the same effect as a permanent restriction on the number of calories.

This data forms the basis of the theory of intermittent fasting.[1] The first human studies[2] are recent and, each time, intermittent fasting has had a positive effect on health markers such as weight, cholesterol, blood pressure, and blood sugar levels. Long-term trials are under way to evaluate the effectiveness of calorie restriction on people who do not suffer from obesity.

How to use this book

1 Reread the advice about the diet.

2 Prepare your meals with the help of the suggested recipes.

3 Eventually follow the one-month program suggested at the end of the book: one month of menu plans based on the principles of intermittent fasting, alternating Fast-Day recipes and suggestions for healthy and balanced meals on the other five days. We are convinced it is possible to create and enjoy delicious and easy seasonal menus, and enhance your health and vitality at the same time.

.... Did you know? ....

Some say that intermittent fasting simulates the way we ate in prehistoric times, with periods of abundance alternating with times when food was rationed. In many cultures, periods of fasting are practiced for spiritual reasons, but also to enhance physical health.

[1] J.E. Brown, M. Mosley and S. Aldred, "Intermittent fasting: a dietary intervention for prevention of diabetes and cardiovascular disease?," *British Journal of Diabetes & Vascular Disease*, 13: 68, 2013.

[2] Anton, S., "Fasting or caloric restriction for healthy aging," *Christiaan Leeuwenburgh Experimental Gerontology*, vol. 48, no. 10: 1003–1005, October 2013.

THE PRINCIPLE
OF THE DIET

Our diet is structured over the course of a week. It includes two days when food intake shouldn't exceed 500 calories per day for women and 600 calories for men. These two days are called Fast Days. They aren't necessarily taken together. On the other five days, called the Non-Fast Days, the idea is to eat normally.

How does it work?

On two days each week (not necessarily in a row), calorie intake is reduced to 25 percent of the normal intake. To maintain a stable weight, a woman needs an average of 2000 calories per day and a man 2500 calories. So, on Fast Days, a woman should consume no more than 500 calories and a man 600. Why 25 percent? Numerous studies on total fasting (no food for 24 hours or more) or calorie restriction (eating less on a permanent basis) show that the 25 percent rule is the maximum amount of food that can be consumed without losing the benefits of fasting. This is the threshold at which studies on animals start to show positive effects on health. Then, on the Non-Fast Days, while you need to be sensible (don't overcompensate by going up to 150 percent!), you can easily satisfy your appetite.

A SIMPLE DIET
Studies show that many diets are difficult to follow because they require you to limit your calorie intake every day. This is why it is so difficult to lose weight in a sustainable way. With intermittent fasting, your intake is limited only on two days. On the other days, you can relax and enjoy tasty little dishes that are richer but still healthy and balanced.

A FLEXIBLE DIET
You can choose and plan your Fast Days according to your own schedule. They don't need to be consecutive and you can even organize them at the last minute, in case your plans change.

A DIET THAT LETS YOU EAT
The 5:2 diet is not about eliminating certain food groups, eating diet foods, or taking expensive dietary supplements. Over time, the meals on your Non-Fast Days will naturally become lower in fat and higher in vegetables and proteins. We believe that to get the full benefit from intermittent fasting, you should make healthy and balanced meals on your Non-Fast Days as well.

Speaking for ourselves, around 80 percent of the time we eat balanced meals, and the rest of the time we eat completely freely, for pleasure! Fatty and overly sugary foods don't often make it past the doors of our homes, but we allow ourselves to be more decadent during dinners with friends, celebrations, and holidays. It's up to you to find the method and rhythm that suits you best so that the majority of your meals are healthy and high in essential nutrients.

A healthy diet is not an end in itself but a path to follow. It's just a target. The emphasis should be on health rather than on weight—studies show that people who adopt this attitude manage their weight better. Make a list of five reasons, apart from weight, why you'd like to try intermittent fasting, and keep them within easy reach. So, what are they? More energy, a glowing complexion, a sharper mind? Your personalized list will help to keep you motivated.

THE BENEFITS
OF INTERMITTENT FASTING

The 5:2 diet promotes weight loss, but this is not the only positive effect. It improves your state of health on several levels.

Weight loss

One of the main motivations for intermittent fasting is weight loss.

1 Restricting intake to 500 calories for women and 600 calories for men two days a week (with a normal diet on the other five days) amounts to 3000–3800 fewer calories per week. Considering that 1 pound of fat has a caloric value of around 3500, it is possible to lose just over 1 pound (half a kilo) per week. The good news is that many people lose even more weight. It's recommended that you practice intermittent fasting over an extended period of time, because it seems to encourage the body to burn fat even more efficiently. After a month, the average weight loss is just under 7 pounds (3 kilograms) for women and up to a little over 11 pounds (5 kilograms) for men. In addition, intermittent fasting increases the production of a tiny gene called SIRT1, which helps accelerate weight loss by reducing fat storage and activating lipid metabolism.

2 Another effect of intermittent fasting is that the body gets accustomed to being satisfied with smaller portions, which allows us to become aware of what we really need to feed ourselves. You can also become an expert in calorie counting, which will be useful for Non-Fast Days.

3 Other people have told us that intermittent fasting enables them to experience a feeling of hunger without feeling like they're starving and reacting immediately to their symptoms by eating. In the obesogenic environment we live in, food is omnipresent. Intermittent fasting conditions you to tolerate this feeling of hunger in the short term until the next meal.

4 Our concept of the "Super 500" dishes means the body doesn't become nutrient-deficient while fasting. That way, the body doesn't compensate afterwards by storing richer foods.

Improved health markers

1 Studies on animals indicate that a reduction in calories leads to a slight tension in the cells and the body in general. This tension seems to help cells protect themselves against wear and tear. Intermittent fasting promotes a process called autophagy, which enables cells to repair themselves by themselves and eliminate any toxins more efficiently.

2 Research has shown that this process helps to reduce inflammation. Inflammation is connected to a number of medical conditions such as cerebral degeneration, type 2 diabetes, cardiovascular disease, cancer, and other age-related diseases. It seems that intermittent fasting reduces inflammatory markers, particularly by improving the way the body regulates its blood sugar levels, due to a better response of the cells to insulin.

3 Studies have shown that intermittent fasting helps to lower cholesterol levels.

If your goal is truly to optimize and improve some of these health markers, you should also pay attention to what you eat on the Non-Fast Days. Without going to the trouble of counting calories, you should try to eat as healthily as possible.

The fight against aging

When people talk about the fight against aging, we usually think of anti-wrinkle creams that are supposed to give you a radiant complexion, or even Botox and cosmetic surgery. Not to come across as prophets of doom, but we also need to think about our brains and the risks of dementia and similar age-related diseases. Studies show that intermittent fasting tends to stimulate brain function and reduce the risk of injury or illness. It stimulates the production of protective factors that enhance neuronal function and helps the brain resist aging and preserve its functions. According to studies on animals, it protects neurons against Alzheimer's, Parkinson's, and Huntington's diseases, and against strokes.[3]

The most visible aspect of aging is the skin. The older it gets, the more vulnerable it is to damage caused by internal or external toxins. Intermittent fasting helps cells to repair and renew themselves more quickly. It increases the production of a substance called somatropin hormone (STH), which helps strengthen skin functions, muscles, tendons, ligaments, and bones. Somatropin also improves skin by reducing wrinkles and fine lines.

Who should not practice intermittent fasting?

Even though we fully support the principle of intermittent fasting, it is important to stress that this diet is not recommended for certain groups of people for various reasons:

- Children and adolescents.
- People suffering from diseases such as diabetes or other problems concerning the control of blood sugar levels.
- People suffering from digestive disorders such as irritable bowel syndrome, Crohn's disease, or ulcerative colitis.
- People suffering from depression or chronic stress or who are naturally anxious.
- People who have shown signs of having an eating disorder.
- People taking certain medications, in particular diabetes medications or beta-blockers.
- Pregnant or breastfeeding women.
- Elite athletes.
- People suffering from obesity.

If in doubt, we recommend consulting your doctor. And even if you don't follow the dietary restrictions of Fast Days, you can still enjoy our delicious recipes and menu ideas for the five Non-Fast Days.

---

3 M.P. Mattson, W. Duan and Z. Guo, "Meal size and frequency affect neuronal plasticity and vulnerability to disease: cellular and molecular mechanisms," *Journal of Neurochemistry*, 84(3): 417–31, February 2003.

.... Did you know? ....

The body produces two hormones for regulating blood sugar levels. Blood sugar needs to be strictly controlled because if it is abnormally high, the sugar can cause damage to the body's organs and cells. Insulin is a hormone that's released in response to high blood sugar levels. It helps move the sugar (glucose) from the bloodstream into the cells, where it is stored or used as energy. Glucagon, on the other hand, is a hormone released in response to low blood sugar levels. It helps move the sugar stored in the cells into the bloodstream.

Are you lost? Simply put: insulin promotes fat storage whereas glucagon helps to burn it. Intermittent fasting helps cells respond more efficiently to insulin, preventing it from being released in too large a quantity. Intermittent fasting, therefore, helps you to burn fat!

THE
STRUCTURE
OF FAST DAYS

On the Fast Days calorie intake is restricted, but these days are nothing to worry about. By learning to understand different foods and what they provide you, you'll sail through these days.

When should I eat?

The advantage of intermittent fasting is that you can structure your Fast Days to suit you. You can choose to have breakfast, then a snack at noon and a light dinner, or you can skip a meal and divide the calories between lunch and dinner or breakfast and dinner. You can also try to have only one meal a day, but we'd advise you not to attempt this option until you get used to intermittent fasting.

Our menu suggestions for Fast Days are based on two meals a day, lunch and dinner, for the following reasons:

- Breakfast tends to stimulate the appetite (it does ours anyway!).
- Breakfast is probably the easiest meal to skip.
- The fasting period is naturally extended if you skip breakfast, so you can burn a greater amount of fat. If you finish dinner at around 9 pm the night before and don't eat before 1 pm the next day, this amounts to a 16-hour fast.

Is it really healthy to skip breakfast?

Past studies have shown that people who eat breakfast tend to have healthier eating habits (exercising more, eating more vegetables and less sugar) than those who skip breakfast. Though it has been recommended in the past to "never skip breakfast," we have learned that it is not necessarily the fact of eating breakfast that guarantees better health. Eating breakfast does not kickstart metabolism or give any extra health benefits on its own.

Do the two Fast Days need to be together?

The two Fast Days don't necessarily have to be in a row. We recommend (for the more adventurous) practicing intermittent fasting on two nonconsecutive days for the first two weeks, then two consecutive days for the last two weeks. The difference is not necessarily noticeable in terms of weight loss, but it means the Fast Days are over with sooner. Some people actually find it easier to keep going with their fasting once they've started. The body needs to get used to fasting. This is difficult for some, but after three to four days, the body gets used to experiencing hunger without insisting on food. It's possible to live with the feeling of hunger with no problem. After a few weeks of practice, it's no longer a hardship—it's a way of life!

........What are calories?..........

Calories are a measure of the energy in food and drinks. We use them to supply energy to our body, or to store the energy for later use. The caloriesin the different food groups and alcohol are counted in the following way:

1 g fat = 9 calories
1 g protein = 4 calories
1 g carbohydrate = 4 calories
1 g alcohol = 7 calories

The foods that are richest in calories are fats, followed by alcohol!

What should I eat?

QUALITY AND QUANTITY

On the Fast Days, every calorie counts. You really need to be conscious of the quantities of food you consume. We recommend eating good-quality food on these days. You can, of course, use up your recommended calories by eating a few squares of chocolate, but that will not give you the nutrients you need to help manage your hunger. To manage your Fast Days easily, we suggest you balance your meals with protein, unrefined carbohydrates, and lots of vegetables.

PROTEINS

Protein-rich foods have a low glycemic index[4], and are therefore digested slowly, helping you feel full. It is essential to eat protein in sufficient quantities on Fast Days. Foods that are high in protein and low in calories include white fish, crustaceans, eggs, and poultry. Legumes in small quantities are also a good source of protein and contain little fat.

STARCHES

Starchy foods (grains, potatoes, rice, pasta) are high in carbohydrates. Whenever possible, we recommend eating whole grains, which contain more fiber than refined (white) grains and have a lower glycemic load (GL). They are a good source of sustainable energy.

FRUITS AND VEGETABLES

Vegetables are generally low in calories and can be eaten in large quantities to fill out meals. They provide lots of vitamins and minerals as well as fiber, which means they're digested more slowly. Their energy is, therefore, released in a measured way. Fruits contain more calories; you can eat them on Fast Days, but pay attention to quantities.

FATS

We don't have anything against "good" fats, which are essential for many bodily processes and functions. According to research, we should eat more omega-3 fatty acids (found in oily fish, nuts, and seeds) and monounsaturated fatty acids (found in olive oil and avocado). These fats can easily be incorporated into meals on the five Non-Fast Days, but should be eaten only in very small amounts on the Fast Days. A teaspoon of vegetable oil, for example, represents about 45 calories and 1/2 oz (15 g) of nuts "costs" 100 calories!

BEVERAGES

We suggest you avoid drinking any alcohol on Fast Days to give your liver a rest. Alcohol is a source of empty calories, and the goal is to optimize your intake of nutrients on fasting days. A 1/2-cup (4–fl oz/125-ml) glass of wine contains about 90 calories.

---

[4] The glycemic index measures how quickly foods are digested. A low index indicates that the food will be digested slowly.

A small can of beer contains about 155 calories. Save those calories for Non-Fast Days instead. You can drink as much water, tea, and herbal tea as you like on Fast Days (without sugar or milk). We recommend limiting caffeine to no more than four cups of coffee per day. People tend to drink more coffee on Fast Days to ease their hunger and compensate for their lack of energy—but be aware that caffeine has a stronger effect on people with an empty stomach, causing palpitations or other symptoms in sensitive individuals. We also advise against diet drinks, which contain artificial ingredients. Water remains the cheapest and healthiest drink! Why not flavor your water naturally with mint leaves, lemon verbena, or lemon slices?

FLAVORFUL MEALS

In our recipes, we use low-calorie but flavor-packed ingredients such as fresh herbs, citrus zest, and spices, because flavorful meals help you enjoy Fast Days. We give preference to cooking methods that preserve the most vitamins and minerals.

---

calorie table

100 CALORIES of raw proteins	100 CALORIES of raw grains	100 CALORIES of raw fruits and vegetables
3½ oz (100 g) chicken breast	1 oz (30 g) rice	1 lb 9 oz (700 g) green leafy vegetables
2¼ oz (60 g) lean beef	1 oz (25 g) quinoa	7 oz (200 g) carrots
4¼ oz (120 g) white fish	1½ oz (40 g) bread	1 lb 2 oz (500 g) cherry tomatoes
1 oz (30 g) lentils	1 oz (25 g) pasta	1 medium banana
½ oz (15 g) almonds	1 oz (30 g) rice vermicelli	7 oz (200 g) berries

Examples of combinations for Fast Days with two meals:
Meal 1 = 3½ oz (100 g) chicken + 1 oz (30 g) rice + 1 enormous salad
Meal 2 = 1 oz (25 g) quinoa + mixed vegetables + ½ oz (15 g) walnuts

tips for Fast Days

One day or another, you'll have trouble fasting. Simply swap days and postpone your fast until later. It's easier to fast on a day when you're working or busy than a day spent at home or with the family. We found that Mondays and Thursdays were the best days for us.

Try to think about other things besides food on fasting days. Above all, don't spend the whole day thinking about what you're going to eat the next day! Make the most of both the Fast Days and the Non-Fast Days.

The first week of intermittent fasting is often the hardest. The second week will already be easier. Choose your days wisely in the first week and make sure you're busy on these days.

Plan your meals.

- Try to eat healthy, nourishing, enjoyable food with maximum nutritional value so you feel satisfied. Give priority to proteins, vegetables, and unrefined grains.
- Avoid empty calories. Alcohol and highly processed or sugary foods are low in nutrients and fiber, and the body absorbs them too quickly. Therefore, you feel hungry again sooner.
- Avoid ready-to-eat precooked meals, especially diet meals, which often hide a lot of refined carbohydrates and salt. Instead, try our everyday and practical "Super 500" recipes!
- Eat fresh foods. Because each calorie counts, consume them in fresh, appetizing, and flavorful meals instead of precooked meals, meal replacements, or high-protein drinks.
- If you really do not have the time or inclination to cook, buy a packet of precooked rice, a few prawns or chickpeas, and a salad—a real gourmet "Fast" meal (you can find all the calorie information on the packets).

Stay hydrated. This is an important point. In effect, since your food intake is limited on Fast Days, the amount of water provided by food is also reduced. Your body can also confuse hunger and thirst. Drink a glass of water with each meal and whenever you feel hunger coming on.

Find the right rhythm. One of the advantages of intermittent fasting is its flexibility, so make the most of it.

Do you have trouble getting to sleep at night on Fast Days?

We have found that the combination of protein and vegetables at dinnertime can disturb sleep. This problem seems to be solved by adding a small amount of unrefined carbohydrates (brown rice or quinoa to the meal). In effect, carbohydrates stimulate the absorption of certain proteins that are used to make serotonin, a neurotransmitter that helps promote the sleep cycle.

At the start, weigh the ingredients until you have a better idea of portion sizes.

Are you hungry?

- Try drinking a glass of water and waiting 20 minutes. Your body can sometimes confuse hunger and thirst.
- Distract yourself: take a walk, go back to your work, chat with a friend, read a magazine.
- Learn how to recognize hunger and tell yourself it will eventually pass. You won't die of hunger from waiting an hour or two before eating.
- Allow yourself a little snack—for example, 1/2 oz (15 g) raw nuts or a basket of fresh berries. You can then either adjust the other meals to take the snack into account or have a fasting day with a few more calories—this snack will add about 100 calories to your daily intake.

What should I do if I'm having trouble coping with a Fast Day?

We have already indicated that intermittent fasting is not advisable for some people. If you experience strong headaches or excessive tiredness or if you feel weak or irritable on Fast Days, we advise you to stop fasting. Some people, especially those who graze a lot throughout the day, can find it difficult to limit themselves to two small meals.

We suggest you start with a month of preparation, using the menus we've developed for the Non-Fast Days, so you get used to eating only three balanced meals a day. Our meals contain slow-release carbohydrates and healthy proteins that will help you feel full. When you feel ready, you can begin the fasting program.

MEALS
ON FAST DAYS

On Fast Days, women are allowed 500 calories. It's up to you how you allocate them throughout the day.

The "Super 500" concept

Our personal experience only confirms the difficulty of preparing balanced meals on Fast Days. We don't have the time or inclination to spend hours in the kitchen on fasting days, especially as this encourages us to nibble—so we have developed a unique system called "Super 500" that provides for two meals per fasting day. The advantage is that you just cook one 500-calorie dish, then divide the "pot" into two portions that you eat whenever you want. We've tried to make these meals as tasty and satisfying as possible: you may not even realize that it's a Fast Day! This method minimizes temptations.

The "Super 500" recipes

In this book you'll find 30 "Super 500" recipes to choose from based on the season and on what you have in your refrigerator.

The number of calories in these recipes has been carefully designed to provide maximum flavor and nutrients while rationing the calorie content. In the case of some recipes, we have devised extra ingredients to add to the second meal for maximum variety in the day. These seasonal meals are fresh and easy to prepare, and use the following ingredients:

- Whole grains such as quinoa and black rice: they provide a good dose of fiber, which is digested slowly and produces a feeling of fullness for longer.
- High-quality lean proteins such as chicken, fish, beans, and lentils, which provide essential nutrients while containing only a moderate number of calories.
- Good fats in the form of nuts, seeds, and oils.
- Lots of fresh vegetables, which provide essential vitamins and minerals, but also color, texture, and flavor.

These meals allow you to optimize your intake of essential nutrients and feel full of vitality. They also allow the body and mind to get used to eating less on the Non-Fast Days.

Note: You can also make the "Super 500" recipes in larger quantities for Non-Fast Days!

Breakfast

On Fast Days, most people prefer to skip breakfast and save their quota of calories for a light lunch and dinner. This practice has the advantage of extending the fasting period. But if you'd prefer to keep breakfast, it's perfectly acceptable to do so.

Breakfast suggestions for Fast Days (about 100 calories):
- 3½ oz (100 g) berries + 3½ oz (100 g) of plain low-fat yogurt (for those who can't manage without dairy products)
- 1 medium egg (hard-boiled or cooked without added fat) + a salad of tomato and arugula or sliced vegetables
- 7 oz (200 g) fresh fruit salad (avoid pineapple, bananas, and grapes)
- ½ oz (15 g) mixed nuts (almonds, hazelnuts, walnuts, macadamia nuts, etc.)

Other options are available if you plan on having a more substantial breakfast (about 200 calories) and thus prefer to skip another meal:
- 1 omelette (2 eggs) with mixed vegetables + a few salad leaves
- 1 oz (30 g) low-sugar cereal (such as All-Bran) + 3½ fl oz (100 ml) skim milk + 1 small apple cut into wedges
- 1 slice (1 oz/30 g) whole-grain bread + 1 slice (1 oz/30 g) medium-fat cheese + 1½ oz (40 g) cherry tomatoes

Tip: Berries are low in sugar but high in antioxidants such as anthocyanins. When they're out of season, you can use frozen berries.

Lunch and dinner: your choice of recipes

We have also designed around 30 tasty recipes ranging from 100–300 calories, so you can pick and choose for yourself. You can put together your own Fast Day menu based on what you like, what's at the market, and what's in your refrigerator, but also with an eye toward the family or friends you'll be sharing your meal with.

THE GOLDEN RULES
FOR THE NON-FAST DAYS

01

Eat balanced meals for lunch and dinner that contain unrefined carbohydrates (whole grains), proteins, and vegetables.

What proportions of the different food groups should we eat? It's a subject of much debate, but as a general rule we think that you should have roughly the following proportions at each meal: 25% protein + 25% whole grains + 50% fruit and vegetables.

Eat whole grains as much as possible and limit your consumption of refined grains (white bread and white rice). Give preference to fish, poultry, beans, and nuts for your protein. Limit red meat to two or three times a week. Limit bacon, sausages, and other cured meats as well; they contain much too much saturated fat and salt.

02

Include a small portion of protein in your breakfast (yogurt, nuts, cheese).

Studies show that breakfasts that contain a little protein provide lasting energy for the morning and help you to avoid snacking! Good sources of protein for breakfast include dairy products, seeds, nuts, and lean meats.

03

Eat more than five vegetables and fruits a day. Five is the minimum!

General nutritional advice suggests that we should eat at least five fruits and vegetables a day. We recommend going up to four or five servings of vegetables and two or three servings of fruit a day. Why more vegetables than fruit? Vegetables are slightly more nutritious, but above all they contain less sugar. It's important to eat the largest variety of foods possible to optimize your nutritional intake. (Fries and chips don't count as a vegetable! We put them in the starches category.) As a guide, one serving corresponds to approximately 2¾ oz (80 g).

04

Eat "good" fats.

Fats are essential for your health. They are used to make hormones and neurotransmitters and to keep our cells healthy. Diets that are very low in fat are not healthy. We believe it's better to eat real foods that are naturally low in fat.

For example, what's the difference between a no-fat yogurt and a full-fat yogurt? No-fat equals 40 calories, while full-fat equals 61 calories and 3 g fat. But the full-fat yogurt tastes so much better!

Nevertheless, if you can't manage without dairy products on Fast Days, choose "light" products so you don't load up on calories. It's okay to do this occasionally.

We prefer butter and monounsaturated fats such as olive oil for cooking or dressing.

Precious omega-3 fatty acids are provided by two servings of oily fish per week and a daily ration of nuts and seeds.

The menus proposed in this book are low in saturated fats because they contain limited amounts of red meat and dairy products.

The fats to avoid at all costs are trans fats and hydrogenated fats. Many studies have found a connection between these fats and an increased risk of health problems such as inflammation, cancer, and even infertility. Trans fats and hydrogenated fats are solid oils produced artificially from vegetable oils. They are sometimes found in precooked meals and processed foods. Read labels carefully! Oxidized fats form when oils are heated to a temperature that is too high. This damages the oil and changes its structure, transforming it into a compound that can cause inflammation in the body.

05

Stay hydrated. Water is really the best health drink.

You can drink as much water as you like. For coffee and tea lovers, there's good news—recent studies have shown that they are, in fact, good for your health, especially if you don't add sugar. They contain phytochemicals called polyphenols and other substances that potentially improve your health. That being said, high levels of caffeine can increase blood pressure and cause insomnia among the most sensitive individuals. We need to be aware of our limits!

06

Beware of sugar! Limit sweets to twice a week.

Everyone knows that fat isn't good but we often forget that sugar can be a real poison. Too much sugar increases the risk of obesity, type 2 diabetes, and dental problems. Sugar offers very little in the way of nutrients. Read labels carefully: look for the sugar content percentages. If a food contains more than 10 percent sugar, it is very sugary.

07

Try not to eat between meals.

By eating well-balanced meals, you can avoid snacking. The risk with snacking is eating foods that are unhealthy. And at the end of the day you forget everything you've nibbled on! The recommendation is to limit yourself to two or three meals a day (some people don't eat breakfast) plus one snack if necessary in the afternoon.

08

Limit alcohol to no more than six glasses of wine and/or beer per week. One wine = 1/2 cup (4 fl oz/125 ml).

Current recommendations regarding alcohol consumption indicate a maximum of 14 units per week for women and 21 for men. It's also recommended not to drink alcohol at all on one or two days a week to let the liver recover.

We have already suggested not drinking alcohol on Fast Days. On days when you are drinking alcohol, the sensible option is to limit consumption to no more than two units for women and no more than three units for men.

What is a unit of alcohol?

A unit of alcohol corresponds to 1/4 fl oz (10 ml) of pure alcohol by volume, or 1/3 oz (8 g) in weight. For example, a unit of alcohol is roughly equivalent to:

- 8 fl oz (230 ml) beer
- 3/4 fl oz (25 ml) spirits (40% alcohol)
- 1/2 cup (4 fl oz/125 ml) wine (12% alcohol)

And don't forget the most important thing: enjoy what you eat! Good food is both a pleasure and a privilege. Meals should be enjoyed and savored. You might not always eat within the rules at every meal or on every day, but try to strike a balance over the course of the week. Your meals shouldn't become a chore or a source of guilt. Eating is a pleasure! And eating without hang-ups is a big step towards wellness.

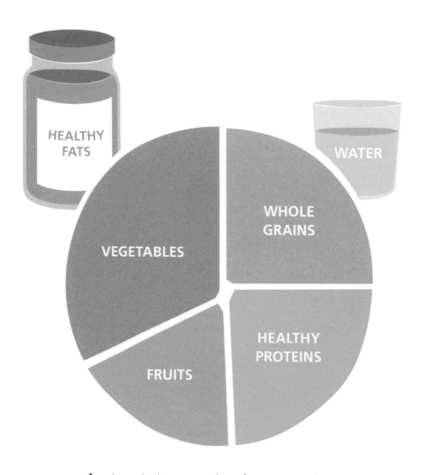

For lunch and dinner, eat balanced meals containing unrefined carbohydrates (whole grains), proteins, and vegetables, with some fruit. Drink plenty of water to stay hydrated, and include small amounts of healthy fats.

ADVICE
FOR THE NON-FAST DAYS

An example of a 2000-calorie day

Breakfast:
Whole-grain toast, fruit salad, plain yogurt, and tea/coffee.

Lunch:
Spicy chickpea salad (page 162), green salad with herbs (page 111), cheese, and bread. Dessert.

Afternoon snack:
1 piece of fruit and ½ oz (15 g) nuts.

Dinner:
Energy soup (page 152), fish tartare (page 172), and a glass of wine.

Don't forget to keep an eye on the quality and quantity of the foods you eat on Non-Fast Days.

....

A note on dairy products

Milk, yogurt, and cheese are important sources of calcium. We recommend one to three servings per day. Cheese, which is high in fat, should be consumed in moderate amounts. We prefer plain yogurt over fruit yogurts, which contain too much sugar. It's better to sweeten your yogurt yourself with fresh fruit or a dash of honey.

We do not recommend nonfat dairy products, especially on the Non-Fast Days. In dairy products, fats add flavor, enhance the feeling of fullness, and contain the valuable fat-soluble vitamins A and D.

Suggestions for "healthy" desserts

Can desserts be healthy? Of course. Certainly you should limit cakes and other very sugary desserts to one or two times per week, but you can enjoy fruit-based desserts on Non-Fast Days, such as Greek-style yogurt, fresh fruit, and nuts; baked fruit gratins (apricots and plums lend themselves beautifully to these); fruit salad; and compotes and crumbles.

Among the desserts reserved for special occasions, chocolate mousse deserves a special mention (dark chocolate is an important source of magnesium and flavonols, an antioxidant phytochemical that

protects cells). We are also very fond of different kinds of crumbles. Especially good are those made with rolled oats and chestnut flour.

Other useful tips include using whole-wheat flour to make cakes. Also note that in many desserts, the amount of sugar can be reduced by half without changing the taste or texture.

The benefits of the Mediterranean diet combined with intermittent fasting

We recommend you follow a Mediterranean-style diet to optimize health benefits such as controlling blood sugar levels, cholesterol, and blood pressure. This diet includes lots of fruits and vegetables, lean proteins, nuts, legumes, seeds, and whole grains. It also includes good fats (olive oil) and omega-3 fatty acids, while limiting the saturated fats found in red meat and especially in highly processed foods (such as cakes and desserts).

Studies show that this type of diet is effective in reducing the risk of cardiovascular disease and cerebral degeneration. The combination of intermittent fasting and a Mediterranean diet can not only contribute to weight loss but can also reduce the future risk of disease. Isn't that motivation enough?

.... Did you know? ....

Our digestive system is sometimes called the "second brain." It contains a whole network of neurons that communicate with the nervous system. These neurons and neurotransmitters send a message to the brain 30 minutes after eating: "I'm not hungry anymore!" By eating more slowly, the digestive system will be able to tell the brain that you've eaten enough before it's too late!

Question: How long does it take food to reach the stomach? Answer: 5 to 6 seconds once it's been chewed and swallowed!

QUESTIONS
& ANSWERS

Is intermittent fasting bad for your health?

The latest studies show that partial fasting produces health benefits. This way of eating is quite close to the way our ancestors ate. At times they would experience periods of abundance, while at other times food would be rationed. That's why our body is made to cope with this way of eating. Most of us eat too much and too often! It is important to manage fasting in a sensible way by following the 5:2 diet. You should also make sure that you drink enough water. If in doubt, talk to your doctor about practicing intermittent fasting.

Why is the calorie intake capped at no more than 25 percent?

This is the threshold at which studies on animals have shown positive effects on health.

Why are men allowed to eat more than women?

Men are more muscular than women, so their metabolic rate is slightly higher. On average, a man needs 2500 calories per day to maintain his weight, while a woman needs 2000.

Do I really have to keep within 500/600 calories a day? What if I go over a bit?

It's not the end of the world if you eat 600–700 calories on the Fast Days, but try not to go over. Any extra calories will have an effect on your weight loss, but studies on animals still show improved health markers when the calorie restriction was only 30 percent.

Can I add milk or sugar to my tea/coffee?

You can add milk or sugar to your coffee, but don't forget to factor these calories into your daily total. For health reasons, we recommend that you reduce your intake of sugar as much as possible or replace sugar with a natural sweetener like stevia.

Can I shift my mealtimes?

Once again, the advantage of the 5:2 diet is its flexibility. As long as you don't go over 500–600 calories in 24 hours, you can eat whenever you want. Some prefer to eat one meal during the day, while others choose to keep breakfast and lunch but skip dinner. To obtain the best results, we suggest you try to have 16 hours in a row of total fasting, and therefore to make your meals at least eight hours apart (for example, 1 pm to 9 pm or 8 am to 4 pm).

Why am I not losing weight on the diet?

The most common reason people don't lose weight on the 5:2 diet is that they overcompensate on the Non-Fast Days. We insist on the importance of eating healthy and balanced meals on the Non-Fast Days. It's not about counting calories, but remembering that high alcohol consumption combined with fatty and sugary foods is likely to put you over your daily calorie intake.

We recommend keeping a food diary of what you eat, which is very helpful for keeping your goals in mind!

Can I adapt some of the recipes in the book?

Of course you can adapt our recipes. This is why we have detailed the number of calories of each ingredient and added calorie tables for the most commonly eaten foods.

Can I exercise on Fast Days?

You can exercise on Fast Days. In fact, recent studies show that physical activity on an empty stomach (before eating) is more efficient from the point of view of fat loss. As always, start slowly and stop immediately if you feel weak or dizzy.

Should I take vitamin or mineral supplements on Fast Days?

The vitamins and minerals we need are supposed to be supplied through our daily diet, and not by way of supplements. We've aimed to put the maximum amount of nutrients into our Fast Day recipes by using whole grains, proteins, and lots of vegetables.

We have also developed menu suggestions and ideas for making the Non-Fast Days as nutritious as possible. In our opinion, if you follow our menu suggestions, you should get all the nutrients you need. Consult your doctor or nutritionist about specific concerns.

THE MAINTENANCE DIET

At the start of the diet, your weight loss goals need to be realistic and specific. You should aim for a healthy weight that you can maintain rather than an unrealistic goal.

The BMI

The aim of the maintenance diet is to have a normal body mass index (BMI), which is between 18.5 and 25 for both women and men. Body mass index[5] (BMI) is a tool used to calculate whether a person's weight is normal or not. It is calculated by multiplying your weight in pounds by 4.88, then dividing this by your height in feet squared. Alternatively, you can divide your weight in kilograms by your height in meters squared.

For example: Weight = 175 lb (79.4 kg), Height = 6 ft (1.83 m)
175 x 4.88 / (6 x 6) = 23.7 or 79.4 / (1.83 x 1.83) = 23.9
A BMI below 18.4 is considered to be underweight, while a score between 18.5 and 25 is ideal. When an individual's BMI is over 25, he or she is considered to be overweight, and over 30 is considered obese.

However, the BMI is not everything. The amount of body fat is more important than BMI. Fat localized around the abdomen, called visceral fat, is a more meaningful indicator of health than the BMI. The higher the amount of visceral fat, the more vulnerable you are to cardiovascular and metabolic diseases. If your BMI is within the normal range but you have high levels of visceral fat, you may have more health problems than a person whose BMI is higher, but who has less visceral fat. Being slightly overweight (a BMI between 25 and 26.5) does not pose any additional health risks. The problem is that the more the weight goes up, the more fats tend to be stored in the form of visceral fat, which can lead to health problems.

Maintaining your weight loss

It is difficult to obtain precise figures, but according to some studies, 20 percent of people who have lost weight manage to maintain their new weight for at least one year.[6] This means that about 80 percent don't manage this: a totally depressing figure! Losing weight is actually only 40 percent of the battle; maintaining the weight loss is 60 percent of the work. The reason many people put weight back on is simply that they haven't adopted new permanent dietary and behavioral habits to help them maintain their weight. Many current diets effectively concentrate on weight loss. But the key to success is then knowing how to adapt the diet so you don't put the weight back on.

The 5:2 diet and weight maintenance

The 5:2 diet can easily be adapted to weight maintenance mode by shifting from two to one fasting days per week—in other words, by following a 6:1 diet instead of 5:2. There would then only be one Fast Day a week, but your diet should still be healthy and balanced on the other six days.

Some use other strategies, such as following the 5:2 diet for two weeks per month, or following the 5:2 diet after the holidays or during specific times when you feel you've put weight back on.

Once again, the advantage of this diet is its flexibility. It's up to you to find the maintenance mode that suits you best.

How often should I weigh myself?

Some people (and there are lots of them!) weigh themselves every day. For our part, we recommend that you weigh yourself once a week, when you wake up in the morning, without any clothes on. Weight varies every day, especially for women, due to hormonal changes and fluid retention. By weighing yourself once a week, you'll have a more accurate idea of your weight loss.

After the weight loss phase, once you're in maintenance mode, it is especially important to continue to monitor your weight every week so you can respond immediately if needed.

Benefit from the positive aspects of intermittent fasting without losing weight

If you are looking to enhance your health but not trying to lose weight, you can put together meals that are a little more "expensive" in calorie terms on the Non-Fast Days. Thus, you can allow yourself larger portions of foods high in protein, carbohydrates, and nutrients such as avocadoes, nuts, and seeds—and a little more dessert!

---

[5] The BMI is not a suitable measure for children, athletes, or pregnant and lactating women.
[6] Wing, R.R. and Phelan, S., "Long-term weight loss maintenance," *The American Journal of Clinical Nutrition*, 2005.

PHYSICAL
ACTIVITY

Exercise plays a vital role in keeping healthy. Contrary to common belief, exercise alone is not enough to lose weight. But the combination of exercise and the 5:2 diet is ideal for losing weight, maintaining weight, and improving your health.

Intermittent fasting allows you to burn a maximum amount of fat. Combined with regular physical activity, it helps reduce body fat while building lean muscle mass.

The benefits of regular physical activity

IMPROVED INSULIN SENSITIVITY AND OTHER METABOLIC MARKERS

Insulin is an essential hormone for regulating blood sugar (glucose) levels and moving glucose into the cells of the body, where it is either stored or used to produce energy. With insulin-sensitive muscles, the body controls its blood sugar levels more effectively and is more efficient at transporting glucose to muscle cells. Exercise can help regulate cholesterol levels and levels of triglycerides (a type of fat present in the blood).

BUILDING AND MAINTAINING LEAN MUSCLE MASS

Exercise allows you to change your body composition. Body composition tells you more about overall health than weight alone. Fat stored around the stomach and internal organs (visceral fat) is bad for your health. Exercise helps reduce this stored fat. Muscles also burn a little more energy than fat—not enough for the difference to be significant in terms of weight loss, but probably enough to help maintain it.

PROTECTING AND STRENGTHENING BONES

Our peak bone mass is reached in early adulthood. Regular exercise allows us to maintain this bone mass and reduce the risk of osteoporosis at a later age, because physical activity helps strengthen and protect bones.

STRESS MANAGEMENT

Exercise reduces stress and releases endorphins, a natural chemical produced by the brain to reduce pain and produce a sense of well-being.

What sort of exercise should I do and how often?

Current recommendations advise adults to be active every day and ideally to have a combination of moderate- and vigorous-intensity activities throughout the week. But the essential thing is to do an exercise you like on a consistent basis, and try new activities from time to time.

VIGOROUS INTENSITY ACTIVITIES
Running, team sports (basketball, soccer), dancing, aerobics

MODERATE INTENSITY ACTIVITIES
Brisk walking, cycling, swimming

STRENGTH TRAINING ACTIVITIES
Yoga, Pilates, weight training

If you haven't done any exercise for a long time, talk about it with your doctor before starting an exercise program. If you're starting an exercise program, you might need to shorten the length of each session at first, then gradually increase them to the recommended 30 minutes.

In the end, we need to find activities that suit us and have fun doing them! Exercise shouldn't ever be torture. Try to move more in everyday life. This can be simple as getting off the train one stop earlier than usual, using a Pilates ball instead of a chair, or getting out of your desk chair every hour for a five-minute walk. Taken together, these small actions make a difference. Exercise contributes to health, strength, and vitality!

CALORIE

tables

TABLE I
GREEN VEGETABLES
calories per 3½ oz (100 g)

baby salad leaves
24 (100)

baby spinach
14 (59)

artichokes
34 (142)

English peas
(shelled)
80 (335)

zucchini
17 (71)

Swiss chard
14 (59)

cucumbers
12 (50)

fennel
31 (130)

green beans
31 (130)

broccoli
34 (142)

leeks
56 (234)

cabbage
20 (84)

asparagus
24 (100)

TABLE 2

VEGETABLES

calories per 3½ oz (100 g)

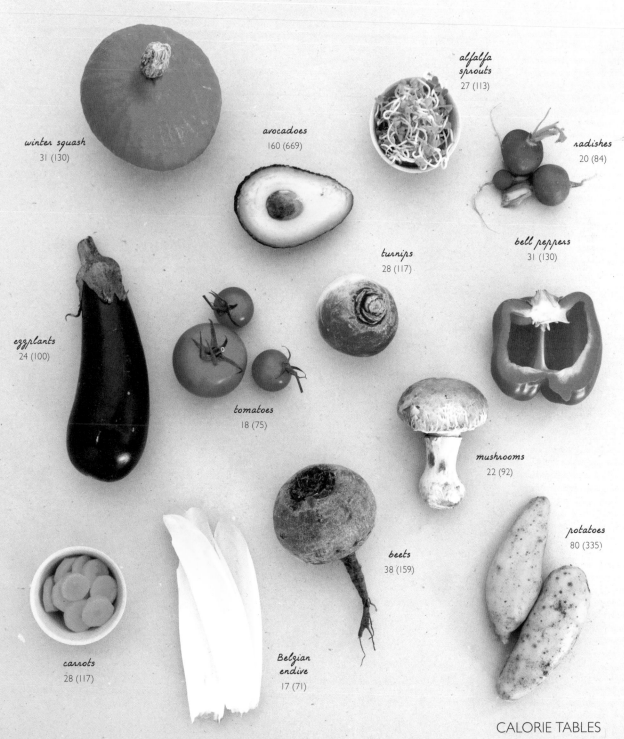

alfalfa
sprouts
27 (113)

avocadoes
160 (669)

radishes
20 (84)

winter squash
31 (130)

bell peppers
31 (130)

turnips
28 (117)

eggplants
24 (100)

tomatoes
18 (75)

mushrooms
22 (92)

beets
38 (159)

potatoes
80 (335)

carrots
28 (117)

Belgian
endive
17 (71)

TABLE 3

LEGUMES & TOFU
UNCOOKED
calories per 3½ oz (100 g)

chickpeas
370 (1548)

black beans
340 (1423)

tofu
120 (502)

red lentils
332 (1389)

French green
(Le Puy) lentils
352 (1473)

kidney beans
338 (1414)

TABLE 4

STARCHES
UNCOOKED
calories per 3½ oz (100 g)

bread
320 (1339)

oat bran
246 (1029)

spelt
338 (1414)

bulgur
344 (1439)

spelt couscous
342 (1431)

pearl barley
352 (1473)

dried rice vermicelli
362 (1515)

kasha (roasted buckwheat)
345 (1443)

cellophane noodles
331 (1385)

quinoa
380 (1590)

millet
378 (1582)

rice
350 (1464)

pasta
344 (1439)

couscous
376 (1573)

TABLE 5

FRUITS

calories per 3½ oz (100 g)

grapes
67 (280)

bananas
89 (372)

limes (juice)
40 (167)

apples
52 (218)

raspberries
53 (222)

melons
28 (117)

plums
46 (192)

mangoes
65 (272)

strawberries
33 (138)

oranges
47 (197)

figs
74 (310)

pineapples
50 (209)

pears
57 (238)

blueberries
57 (238)

peaches
39 (163)

lemons (juice)
40 (167)

TABLE 6
DAIRY PRODUCTS
calories per 3½ oz (100 g)

low-fat milk
50 (209)

ricotta cheese
138 (577)

soy cream
174 (728)

yogurt
70 (293)

parmesan cheese
440 (1841)

crème fraîche
293 (1226)

TABLE 7

CONDIMENTS

calories per ⅛ oz (5 g) or 1 teaspoon (5 ml)

preserved
lemon (½)
9 (38)

vinegar
2 (8)

ground
cinnamon
6 (25)

chiles
5 (21)

mustard
4 (17)

kaffir lime
leaves
1 (4)

fresh ginger
3 (13)

ground
cumin
8 (33)

soy sauce
5 (21)

fennel seeds
17 (71)

caper
berries
2 (8)

TABLE 8
OILS, NUTS & SEEDS
calories per ⅛ oz (5 g) or 1 teaspoon (5 ml)

hazelnuts
31 (130)

flaxseed
27 (113)

butter
35 (146)

*pepitas
(pumpkin seeds)*
22 (92)

pine nuts
28 (117)

vegetable oil
45 (188)

chia seeds
30 (126)

*black or white
sesame seeds*
28 (117)

almonds
29 (121)

TABLE 9

PROTEINS

calories

Meat per 3½ oz (100 g) raw	
Lamb	156 (653)
Beef tenderloin	150 (628)
Beef steak	136 (569)
Ground beef (95% lean)	137 (573)
Veal tenderloin	140 (586)
Pork tenderloin	136 (569)
Ham	107 (448)
Chicken breast	120 (502)
Chicken thigh (skinless)	145 (607)

Fish per 3½ oz (100 g) raw	
Sea bass	125 (523)
Cod	80 (335)
Hake	92 (385)
Sea bream	100 (418)
Prawns (shrimp)	80 (335)
Smoked haddock	95 (397)
Pollack	90 (377)
Mackerel	165 (690)
Mussels (with shell)	43 (180)
Red mullet	111 (464)
Scallops	87 (364)
John dory	90 (377)
Salmon	166 (695)
Smoked salmon	180 (753)
Sole	89 (372)
Bluefin tuna	108 (452)

Eggs per egg	
Egg – small	54 (226)
Egg – medium	71 (297)
Egg – large	90 (377)

See individual recipes for alternative fish suggestions.

Chapter 1

SUPER
500
RECIPES

AL DENTE VEGETABLES
& EGG SAUCE

Super
500

SERVES 1

PREPARATION TIME: 20 MINUTES

COOKING TIME: 10 MINUTES

INGREDIENTS	CALORIES
1 LARGE ZUCCHINI, ABOUT 10 OZ (300 G), UNPEELED	50
7 OZ (200 G) FIRM TOMATOES	36
1 FENNEL BULB, ABOUT 10 OZ (300 G)	93
3 LARGE HARD-BOILED EGGS (LESS 1 EGG YOLK)	199
½ BUNCH (1½ OZ/40 G) CILANTRO, CHOPPED	5
½ TEASPOON GROUND CUMIN	2
2 TEASPOONS OLIVE OIL	90
1 LARGE HANDFUL (1 OZ/25 G) ARUGULA, WASHED & CHOPPED	6
TOTAL	481

VARIATION FOR MEN	
3½ OZ (100 G) CANNED TUNA IN WATER, DRAINED AND FLAKED	116
TOTAL	597

GLUTEN-FREE ◆

Preparing my meal

Slice the zucchini into thick rounds. Steam for 10 minutes: it needs to be al dente. Set aside on paper towels. Blanch the tomatoes in boiling water in a heatproof bowl for 10 seconds, then drop them into cold water. Peel the tomatoes and cut them into wedges. Set aside on paper towels. Discard the tough outer layer of the fennel bulb and slice the bulb very thinly. Reserve one of the hard-boiled egg yolks for another purpose. Mash the 2 remaining whole hard-boiled eggs and 1 hard-boiled egg white in a bowl with a fork. Combine the mashed eggs with the cilantro, cumin, 2 tablespoons cold water, and the olive oil. Season with plenty of pepper and a little salt. Arrange the vegetables on a plate, scatter the arugula over the top and dress generously with the egg sauce.

Variation for men: Add the tuna before dressing with the sauce.

It's ready!

Speedy version: Dice the zucchini, tomato, and fennel; mix with the arugula; dress with sauce.

NUTRITIONAL INFO

Eggs are very nutritious and are a perfect Fast Day food. Are you worried about your cholesterol? Eggs do contain cholesterol, but recent studies show that the cholesterol in eggs does not increase cholesterol levels in the blood. Eggs can be eaten as part of a balanced diet.

QUINOA, TOMATOES,
PRESERVED LEMON & FRESH HERBS

Super
500

SERVES 1
PREPARATION TIME: 15 MINUTES
COOKING TIME: 12 MINUTES

INGREDIENTS	CALORIES
1 ZUCCHINI, ABOUT 9 OZ (250 G)	42
½ CUP (3¼ OZ/90 G) QUINOA	331
½ SMALL PRESERVED LEMON	9
1 GREEN ONION	3
16 CHERRY TOMATOES, ABOUT 7 OZ (200 G)	36
1 LITTLE GEM OR BABY ROMAINE LETTUCE HEART	8
1 SMALL BUNCH (2½ OZ/70 G) HERBS (BASIL, CILANTRO, TARRAGON, MINT, CHERVIL)	5
6–7 HAZELNUTS, ABOUT ¼ OZ (10 G)	63
TOTAL	497

VARIATION FOR MEN	
2 ZUCCHINI, ABOUT 18 OZ (500 G)	84
½ CUP PLUS 1 TABLESPOON (3½ OZ/105 G) QUINOA	386
TOTAL	594

GLUTEN-FREE ◆

Preparing my meal

Cut the zucchini into small pieces. Rinse the quinoa and put it in a medium saucepan with twice its volume of boiling salted water (but no oil) and the pieces of zucchini. Allow 7 minutes of cooking time before turning off the heat and letting stand for 5 minutes. Drain. Rinse the preserved lemon under cold running water and remove the seeds, then chop into small pieces. Chop the green onion, tomatoes, lettuce, and herbs. Crush the hazelnuts before toasting them for a few seconds in a dry frying pan over medium-high heat. Combine all the ingredients and season with salt and pepper. Refrigerate before eating.

It's ready!

Tip: Divide into two meals, and eat it cold for the first meal and warmed slightly for the second.

Variation: If you don't have or don't like preserved lemon, you can replace it with the juice of 1 lemon (10 calories). Add according to your taste.

NUTRITIONAL INFO

Fresh herbs are an excellent way to add flavor without calories on your Fast Days! Basil and cilantro are high in vitamin A, a fat-soluble vitamin that's essential for eye and skin health.

MINI FRITTATAS

Super
500

SERVES 1

PREPARATION TIME: 15 MINUTES

COOKING TIME: 18 MINUTES

INGREDIENTS	CALORIES
2 MEDIUM EGGS + 1 EGG WHITE	159
⅞ CUP (2¼ OZ/60 G) OAT BRAN	147
3 TABLESPOONS (1½ OZ/40 G) LOW-FAT FROMAGE BLANC (ALTERNATIVELY, USE QUARK OR GREEK YOGURT)	32
10 CHIVES, SNIPPED	2
3 FLAT-LEAF PARSLEY SPRIGS, CHOPPED	2
2 PINCHES GROUND CUMIN	1
7 OZ (200 G) TOMATOES, DICED	36
½ YELLOW SUMMER SQUASH, ABOUT 4½ OZ (125 G), DICED	21
¼ ONION, ABOUT 1 OZ (25 G), CHOPPED	7
1 TEASPOON OLIVE OIL	45
1½ TEASPOONS (⅛ OZ/5 G) PARMESAN CHEESE SHAVINGS	22
2 HANDFULS (1¾ OZ/50 G) MIXED SALAD LEAVES	12
TOTAL	**486**

VARIATION FOR MEN

3½ OZ (100 G) HAM, TRIMMED OF FAT AND FINELY CHOPPED	108
TOTAL	**594**

Preparing my meal

Whisk the eggs until they're nice and frothy. Gradually add the oat bran and fromage blanc, the chives and parsley, and the cumin. Season with salt and pepper. Beat together vigorously by hand or with an electric mixer. Add the tomatoes, squash, and onion. Heat a few drops of olive oil in a small frying pan. Pour one-third of the mixture into the pan and let it cook over medium heat for 3 minutes. Turn over and cook for another 3 minutes over low heat, covered. Repeat the process twice more for the rest of the mixture. Sprinkle with Parmesan and serve with mixed salad leaves alongside.

Variation for men: Add the ham at the same time as the tomatoes, squash, and onion.

It's ready!

Tip: Depending on your preference or the size of your frying pan, you can make one, two, three, or four frittatas. Make them "to order," if you prefer, and keep the rest of the mixture in the refrigerator.

Variation: Replace the cumin with curry powder, Espelette pepper, chili powder, or red pepper flakes for a spicier version.

This is an excellent recipe for those who can't go without breakfast or who prefer to have three meals when first embarking on Fast Days.

Note from Delphine: I love this recipe because it is super fast, easy to make, and perfect to take to the office, on a picnic, or to my grandmother's house.

HOMEMADE
LASAGNE

Super 500

SERVES 1
PREPARATION TIME: 25 MINUTES
COOKING TIME: 1 HOUR

INGREDIENTS	CALORIES
2 LONG ZUCCHINI, ABOUT 18 OZ (500 G)	84
1 TEASPOON OLIVE OIL	45
1 ONION, ABOUT 3½ OZ (100 G), SLICED	28
7 OZ (200 G) EGGPLANT, DICED	48
7 OZ (200 G) TOMATOES, CHOPPED	36
2/3 CUP (5 FL OZ/150 ML) TOMATO PURÉE	24
3 TABLESPOONS (1½ OZ/40 G) RICOTTA CHEESE	55
5½ OZ (150 G) HAM, TRIMMED OF FAT AND CHOPPED	161
2 BASIL SPRIGS	2
2 LARGE HANDFULS (1¾ OZ/50 G) ARUGULA	12
TOTAL	495

VARIATION FOR MEN	
7 OZ (200 G) HAM, TRIMMED OF FAT AND CHOPPED	204
3½ TABLESPOONS (1¾ OZ/50 G) RICOTTA CHEESE	69
3½ OZ (100 G) MELBA TOAST (ALTERNATIVELY, USE CRISPBREAD OR RUSKS)	39
TOTAL	591

Preparing my meal

Preheat the oven to 350°F (180°C). Slice the zucchini lengthwise into thin slivers and cook them in a medium saucepan of boiling salted water for 1 minute. Set them aside on paper towels. In a frying pan over high heat, warm ½ teaspoon oil; sauté the onion and eggplant for 5 minutes. Add the tomatoes and tomato purée, season with salt and pepper, and simmer over medium heat for 25 minutes. Add the ricotta and ham, stir, and cook for 3 minutes over low heat. In an 8 in x 10½ in (20 cm x 26 cm) baking dish (ideally), lay out a layer of zucchini slices and pour half the sauce mixture over. Arrange a second layer of zucchini on top, then the rest of the mixture and finally the last layer of zucchini. Drizzle with the remaining olive oil and bake in the oven for 25 minutes. Scatter a few basil leaves over and serve with 1 large handful of arugula at each meal.

Variation for men: Crush the Melba toasts into crumbs and sprinkle over the lasagne before cooking.

It's ready!

Tips:

For dinner, you can simply reheat the dish for 5 minutes at 350°F (180°C). You can also eat this dish lukewarm. It's just as good, especially in hot weather.

Double the quantities in this recipe for a satisfying family meal.

On the Non-Fast Days, add 2 tablespoons (½ oz/15 g) grated Parmesan cheese to the ricotta and put 2 tablespoons (½ oz/15 g) grated Parmesan cheese on top of the lasagne with the Melba toast crumbs to brown in the oven.

FRESH & FAST
SALAD

Super
500

SERVES 1

PREPARATION TIME: 20 MINUTES

INGREDIENTS	CALORIES
3½ OZ (100 G) MUSHROOMS	22
½ CUP (2¼ OZ/60 G) DICED AVOCADO	96
1 TABLESPOON LEMON JUICE	3
16 CHERRY TOMATOES, ABOUT 7 OZ (200 G)	36
4 SLICES BRESAOLA, ABOUT 1 OZ (25 G) (ALTERNATIVELY, USE BEEF JERKY OR OTHER DRIED MEAT)	48
½ CUCUMBER, ABOUT 10 OZ (300 G)	36
⅞ CUP (5 OZ/145 G) COOKED OR CANNED CHICKPEAS	161
3½ OZ (100 G) JUICY TOMATOES	18
½ PRESERVED LEMON	9
3½ OZ (100 G) BABY SALAD LEAVES	24
1 SMALL BUNCH (2½ OZ/70 G) HERBS (TARRAGON, CHIVES, CILANTRO, BASIL), CHOPPED	6
½ TEASPOON CRUSHED TOASTED PINE NUTS	39
TOTAL	**498**

VARIATION FOR MEN	
6 SLICES BRESAOLA, ABOUT 1¼ OZ (35 G) (ALTERNATIVELY, USE BEEF JERKY OR OTHER DRIED MEAT)	64
1¼ CUPS (7 OZ/200 G) COOKED OR CANNED CHICKPEAS	247
TOTAL	**600**

GLUTEN-FREE ◆

Preparing my meal

Brush the mushrooms and chop them into small pieces. Combine the mushrooms with the avocado, drizzle with lemon juice, and set aside. Cut the tomatoes into quarters and the bresaola into strips. Peel the cucumber, remove the seeds, and dice. Rinse and drain the chickpeas. Purée the tomatoes in a food processor with the preserved lemon (rinse and remove the seeds first) and a little pepper. Combine the salad leaves with the mushrooms, avocado, tomatoes, chickpeas, bresaola, cucumber, and herbs. If desired, divide into two meals.

First meal: Take half the salad, dress with half the tomato sauce, and sprinkle with half the toasted pine nuts. Season with salt and pepper again, if necessary.

Second meal: Assemble the second portion in the same way.

It's ready!

Tip: This salad is very practical, quick to make and take away. It's perfect for picnics!

Variation

Replace the chickpeas with kidney beans (see page 124 for cooking instructions).

⅔ CUP (4 OZ/113 G) COOKED OR CANNED KIDNEY BEANS	144
TOTAL	**481**

VARIATION FOR MEN	
1 CUP (6 OZ/175 G) COOKED OR CANNED KIDNEY BEANS	225
TOTAL	**562**

BEETS,
MUSHROOMS & FETA

Super
500

SERVES 1

PREPARATION TIME: 30 MINUTES

COOKING TIME: 20 MINUTES

INGREDIENTS	CALORIES
¼ CUP (1½ OZ/40 G) FRENCH LENTILS	141
2½ TABLESPOONS (1 OZ/25 G) QUINOA	93
2 LARGE HANDFULS (1¾ OZ/50 G) BABY SPINACH	12
1⅓ CUPS (7 OZ/200 G) COOKED BEETS, CHOPPED	74
5½ OZ (150 G) MUSHROOMS, BRUSHED AND THINLY SLICED	33
3 SLICES BRESAOLA, ABOUT 1 OZ (24 G), CUT INTO THIN STRIPS (ALTERNATIVELY, USE BEEF JERKY OR OTHER DRIED MEAT)	36
2½ TABLESPOONS (¾ OZ/20 G) FETA CHEESE, CRUMBLED	53
1 BASIL SPRIG, CHOPPED	1
1 SMALL SHALLOT, CHOPPED	7
1 TEASPOON WALNUT OIL	45
TOTAL	495

VARIATION FOR MEN

⅓ CUP (2¼ OZ/60 G) FRENCH LENTILS	212
3 TABLESPOONS (1 OZ/30 G) QUINOA	110
TOTAL	583

GLUTEN-FREE ◆

Preparing my meal

Cook the lentils following the instructions on the packet and let them cool (or rinse them under cold water to stop the cooking and drain). Rinse the quinoa and cook it according to the instructions on page 124. Combine the lentils and quinoa in a bowl. Add the baby spinach, beets, mushrooms, bresaola, feta, basil and shallot. Season with salt and pepper and toss. At serving time, add the walnut oil and toss again, adding more salt and pepper to taste.

It's ready!

Delphine's advice: So the mushrooms retain their freshness, I suggest you slice them very thinly over the plate using a mandoline at the last moment for each meal. They'll stay nice and crisp and be a lovely color.

Variation: If you don't like cooked beet, you can replace it with thinly sliced raw beet or 1¼ cups (6¼ oz/180 g) grated carrots— the calories will be the same.

Speedy tip: If you cook up batches of lentils and quinoa ahead of time and keep them on hand in the fridge, this recipe will be super quick to assemble.

Note from Delphine: Thanks to Chloé for this super, balanced recipe with a touch of indulgence with the feta!

PASTA
& VEGETABLES

SERVES 1

PREPARATION TIME: 30 MINUTES

COOKING TIME: 36 MINUTES

INGREDIENTS	CALORIES
3½ OZ (100 G) FENNEL	31
½ ZUCCHINI, ABOUT 4½ OZ (125 G)	21
½ EGGPLANT, ABOUT 3½ OZ (100 G)	24
3½ OZ (100 G) MUSHROOMS	22
3½ OZ (100 G) BABY SPINACH	24
7 OZ (200 G) TOMATOES	36
1 TEASPOON OLIVE OIL	45
2 PINCHES CAYENNE PEPPER	1
2 PINCHES GROUND CUMIN	1
1 CUP (3 OZ/85 G) PASTA OF YOUR CHOICE	293
TOTAL	**498**

VARIATION FOR MEN	
1¼ CUP (3¾ OZ/110 G) PASTA	380
TOTAL	**585**

Preparing my meal

Prepare the vegetables: Discard the fennel's tough outer layer and chop the fennel, zucchini, eggplant, and mushrooms into bite-sized pieces. Steam the fennel, zucchini, and eggplant for 15 minutes. Process 1 oz (25 g) of the baby spinach in a food processor with the tomatoes, olive oil, some salt and pepper, and 2 tablespoons water. Pour this sauce into a frying pan over medium heat and simmer for 10 minutes. Add the cayenne, cumin, mushrooms, and steamed vegetables, and cook over low heat for 10 minutes. Meanwhile, cook the portion of pasta (half per meal, if dividing into 2 meals) for 1–2 minutes less than the time indicated on the packet. Before draining the pasta, take 1 small ladleful of pasta water and add it to the vegetable sauce. If desired, set aside half of the sauce for a second meal. Drain the pasta and add it to the frying pan. Stir and continue to cook for 1 minute. Serve immediately with half or all the remaining fresh baby spinach mixed in at the last moment. Do the same for the second meal.

It's ready!

Delphine's advice: If you prefer you can cook all the pasta at once and reheat half of it very gently for a second meal—but I'm always afraid of overcooking the pasta, so I do it in two batches!

Variation: You can use quinoa or buckwheat pasta for a gluten-free recipe.

MINESTRONE

Super
500

SERVES 1

PREPARATION TIME: 25 MINUTES

COOKING TIME: 40 MINUTES

INGREDIENTS	CALORIES
2½ TABLESPOONS (1¼ OZ/35 G) PEARL BARLEY	123
3 TABLESPOONS (1¼ OZ/35 G) QUINOA	128
1 SMALL ROSEMARY SPRIG	1
1 GARLIC CLOVE, CHOPPED	4
3 LARGE HANDFULS (2¼ OZ/60 G) BASIL, CHOPPED	3
½ CARROT, ABOUT 1¾ OZ (50 G)	22
½ FIRM ZUCCHINI, ABOUT 4½ OZ (125 G)	21
1 LEEK, PALE PART ONLY, ABOUT 2½ OZ (75 G)	42
½ ONION, ABOUT 1¾ OZ (50 G)	14
1 PINCH CHILI POWDER	1
½ REDUCED-FAT CHICKEN STOCK CUBE	6
1 TEASPOON TOMATO PASTE	9
⅓ CUP (1¾ OZ/50 G) SHELLED PEAS (4½ OZ/125 G IN THEIR PODS)	40
½ CUP (1¾ OZ/50 G) SHELLED FAVA BEANS	44
1½ TEASPOONS (⅛ OZ/5 G) FRESHLY GRATED PARMESAN CHEESE	22
½ TEASPOON BLACK SESAME SEEDS	13
TOTAL	493

VARIATION FOR MEN

6 TABLESPOONS (2¼ OZ/60 G) QUINOA	219
TOTAL	584

Preparing my meal

Rinse the barley and quinoa under cold water and put them in a heavy-bottomed saucepan with 3 cups (24 fl oz/750 ml) cold water. Add the rosemary, garlic, and half the basil. Cook over low heat, covered, for 15 minutes. Prepare the vegetables: Dice the carrot and zucchini, slice the leek into short lengths, and chop the onion. Remove the lid from the saucepan and add the chili powder, the half stock cube, the tomato paste, carrot, peas, leek, and onion. Season with salt and pepper. Replace the lid and cook over low heat for a further 15 minutes. Uncover again, add the zucchini and favas, and cook for a further 10 minutes. Divide into 2 meals, if desired. Serve each portion sprinkled with remaining basil, Parmesan, and black sesame seeds. (Put aside a little of the remaining basil, Parmesan, and sesame seeds for a second serving.) Note that the minestrone should be served runny, not gluey. If necessary, add a little water during cooking so there's always some in the pot.

It's ready!

Delphine's advice: If dividing into two meals, to make sure the second serving isn't overcooked, strain the minestrone once it's cooked and keep the broth separate. Reheat very gently, reincorporating the hot broth. This recipe is ideal to double, triple, or quadruple for the whole family.

Tip: Using a "magic" Microplane grater to grate Parmesan creates flakes of cheese so thin and light that the volume expands without inflating the calories!

NUTRITIONAL INFO

Barley is a good source of beta-glucans, a soluble fiber that helps keep cholesterol levels under control.

WINTER SOUP

Super **500**

SERVES 1

PREPARATION TIME: 25 MINUTES

COOKING TIME: 35 MINUTES

INGREDIENTS	CALORIES
2¾ OZ (80 G) POTATOES	64
3½ OZ (100 G) WINTER SQUASH	31
2¾ OZ (80 G) JERUSALEM ARTICHOKES	58
1 SMALL TURNIP, ABOUT 3½ OZ (100 G)	28
1 LEEK, PALE PART ONLY, ABOUT 2½ OZ (75 G)	42
3½ OZ (100 G) SAVOY CABBAGE	26
½ BUNCH (2½ OZ/75 G) FLAT-LEAF PARSLEY, CHOPPED	5
1¾ OZ (50 G) PORK TENDERLOIN, CHOPPED	68
1½ TEASPOONS (⅛ OZ/5 G) FRESHLY GRATED PARMESAN CHEESE	22
1 TEASPOON HAZELNUT OIL	45
3 TABLESPOONS (1 OZ/30 G) ROASTED BUCKWHEAT (KASHA)	105
TOTAL	494

VARIATION FOR MEN

2½ OZ (75 G) PORK TENDERLOIN	101
⅓ CUP (1¾ OZ/50 G) ROASTED BUCKWHEAT (KASHA)	176
TOTAL	598

GLUTEN-FREE ◆

Preparing my meal

Prepare the vegetables: dice the potatoes, squash, Jerusalem artichokes, and turnip; cut the leek into short lengths; and cut the cabbage into strips. Heat 5 cups (40 fl oz/1.25 liters) salted water in a saucepan over medium heat and add the vegetables, parsley, and pork. Season lightly with pepper. Cook on a low simmer for 30 minutes. Divide into 2 meals, if you like.

First meal: Serve the soup steaming hot with a little Parmesan and the hazelnut oil.

Second meal: Reheat the soup and add the kasha to the boiling soup. It will stay a little crunchy, but it's delicious that way.

It's ready!

Veggie version: Leave out the pork and increase the kasha in the dish.

¼ CUP (1½ OZ/45 G) ROASTED BUCKWHEAT (KASHA)	156
TOTAL	477

VARIATION FOR MEN

½ CUP (2½ OZ/75 G) ROASTED BUCKWHEAT (KASHA)	264
TOTAL	585

Shopping: You'll find kasha (roasted buckwheat) in your local organic supermarket or online.

Delphine's advice: You can certainly prepare the soup using all the ingredients for two meals. But be careful to add only half the kasha for each meal—otherwise, it will be way overcooked for the second meal.

NUTRITIONAL INFO

Kasha is a gluten-free whole grain with a low glycemic index (GI) ranking. It's great for making you feel fuller for longer.

BLACK BEAN
SOUP

Super
500

SERVES 1

PREPARATION TIME: 25 MINUTES

COOKING TIME: 2 HOURS

SOAKING TIME: OVERNIGHT

INGREDIENTS	CALORIES
6 TABLESPOONS (2¾ OZ/80 G) DRIED BLACK TURTLE BEANS	254
3 CUPS (24 FL OZ/750 ML) HOT CHICKEN STOCK, FAT REMOVED	12
½ ONION, ABOUT 1¾ OZ (50 G), CHOPPED	14
½ TEASPOON GROUND CUMIN	2
½ RED CHILE, SEEDED AND FINELY CHOPPED	1
½ GARLIC CLOVE, CHOPPED	2
8 CILANTRO SPRIGS, CHOPPED	3
GRATED ZEST AND JUICE OF ½ ORGANIC LIME	5
3½ OZ (100 G) TOMATOES, DICED	18
½ RED BELL PEPPER, ABOUT 3½ OZ (100 G), DICED	31
2 HANDFULS (1¾ OZ/50 G) BABY SPINACH, COARSELY CHOPPED	12
1 SLICE (1 OZ/25 G) HAM, TRIMMED OF FAT AND CHOPPED	30
½ MEDIUM HARD-BOILED EGG, CHOPPED	35
1 TEASPOON OLIVE OIL	45
TOTAL	464

VARIATION FOR MEN	
½ CUP (3½ OZ/100 G) DRIED BLACK TURTLE BEANS	325
2 SLICES (2 OZ/50 G) HAM, TRIMMED OF FAT AND CHOPPED	60
TOTAL	595

Preparing my meal

Soak the beans in water overnight in the refrigerator. Rinse and drain them. Combine the beans in a medium saucepan with the hot stock, onion, cumin, chile and garlic, half the cilantro, and salt and pepper. Bring to a boil and simmer very gently for 2 hours. Taste the beans: they should melt in your mouth. Add the lime juice and some salt, and purée the soup. Thin it out with a little boiling water, if necessary. Serve each portion in a deep plate or bowl. If you like, divide into 2 meals. For the first serving, add half the tomato, bell pepper, spinach, remaining cilantro, and the lime zest. Set the other half of these ingredients aside for the second serving. Drizzle with a few drops of olive oil when serving.

First meal: Serve with the ham.

Second meal: Serve topped with the egg.

It's ready!

Speedy tip: You can make this soup with canned black beans instead of the dried turtle beans. Simmer 1 cup (8 fl oz/250 ml) stock for 10 minutes with all the other ingredients (garlic, onion, cumin, chile, half the cilantro, salt and pepper) and then purée with the beans.

7 OZ (200 G) CANNED BEANS	264
TOTAL	474

VARIATION FOR MEN	
9 OZ (245 G) CANNED BEANS	323
TOTAL	593

NUTRITIONAL INFO

Legumes are an excellent source of soluble fiber, which helps maintain a healthy digestive system.

MY RATATOUILLE
FOR THE DAY

Super **500**

SERVES 1
PREPARATION TIME: 20 MINUTES
COOKING TIME: 4 HOURS, 5 MINUTES

INGREDIENTS	CALORIES
2 LARGE HANDFULS (1 OZ/30 G) CILANTRO LEAVES	4
1 ONION, ABOUT (3½ OZ/100 G)	28
2 ZUCCHINI, ABOUT 18 OZ (500 G)	84
1 LARGE EGGPLANT, ABOUT 10½ OZ (300 G)	72
1 TEASPOON OLIVE OIL	45
8½ OZ (240 G) CANNED PEELED TOMATOES	50
1 PINCH GROUND CUMIN	1
1 PINCH PAPRIKA	1
1 LARGE RED BELL PEPPER, ABOUT 7 OZ (200 G)	62
1 LARGE YELLOW BELL PEPPER, ABOUT 7 OZ (200 G)	62
1 LARGE EGG	90
TOTAL	499

VARIATION FOR MEN	
2 LARGE EGGS	180
TOTAL	589

GLUTEN-FREE ◆

Preparing my meal

Prepare the vegetables and herbs: Coarsely chop the cilantro, cut the onion into wedges, and cut the zucchini and eggplant into large cubes. In a flame-proof casserole dish over high heat, heat the olive oil and sauté the onion for 5 minutes. Once the onion is lightly browned, add the tomatoes with their juices, zucchini, and eggplant. Season with salt and pepper, and add the cilantro, cumin, and paprika. Cook over very low heat, covered, for 2 hours. Meanwhile, heat the broiler and broil the bell peppers until they are quite black on all sides. Place them in an airtight bag or a plastic container and let them cool, then remove the skin and the seeds. Slice them into strips. After the first 2 hours of cooking the ratatouille, add the peppers and cook uncovered for another 2 hours over very low heat. Watch carefully to make sure it does not burn (take it off the heat if it does). Divide into 2 meals, if desired.

Second meal: Reheat the ratatouille gently. Soft-boil an egg for 5–6 minutes in boiling water, then peel it under cold running water. Serve the ratatouille in a bowl with the egg on top.

Variation for men: Serve with one soft-boiled egg at each meal.

It's ready!

Tip: Make the ratatouille the day before and reheat very gently.

NUTRITIONAL INFO
Cooked tomatoes are a rich source of lycopene, a powerful antioxidant that has been linked with a reduced risk of heart disease and some cancers. Cooked and canned tomatoes actually contain more lycopene than fresh tomatoes!

Note from Delphine: I often make this dish for the whole family, doubling the quantities. My portion size is still ideal, as it's one-quarter of the total weight. Everyone eats the same thing, which makes mealtime much easier.

QUINOA
& WINTER VEGETABLES

Super
500

SERVES 1

PREPARATION TIME: 20 MINUTES

COOKING TIME: 19 MINUTES

INGREDIENTS	CALORIES
½ CUP (2¾ OZ/80 G) QUINOA	294
1 ZUCCHINI, ABOUT 9 OZ (250 G)	42
5½ OZ (150 G) NAPA CABBAGE	18
1 CUP (5½ OZ/150 G) DICED BUTTERNUT SQUASH	75
1–2 PINCHES GROUND CUMIN	1
1 HEAPING TABLESPOON (¼ OZ/10 G) PEPITAS (PUMPKIN SEEDS), CHOPPED	60
GRATED ZEST OF 1 ORGANIC LIME	2
1 LARGE HANDFUL (1 OZ/25 G) ARUGULA	6
TOTAL	498

VARIATION FOR MEN

½ CUP PLUS 1 TABLESPOON (3½ OZ/105 G) QUINOA	386
2 LARGE HANDFULS (1¾ OZ/50 G) ARUGULA	12
TOTAL	596

GLUTEN-FREE ◆

Preparing my meal

Rinse the quinoa and cook it in one and a half times its volume of boiling salted water (but no oil). Pour in the quinoa when the water is boiling and allow 7 minutes to cook it al dente so it can be reheated a little later without overcooking. Turn off the heat and let stand for 5 minutes. Run the quinoa under cold water to stop the cooking, and drain. Meanwhile, dice the zucchini and cut the cabbage into strips. Heat a large frying pan over high heat without adding any oil and cook the vegetables for 5 minutes, stirring frequently. Reduce the heat, add 3 tablespoons water and the cumin, and cook for another 2 minutes, stirring. Season with salt and pepper. Combine the vegetables with the quinoa and add the chopped pepitas. At mealtime, gently reheat one portion, adding 1–2 tablespoons water if necessary. Before eating, sprinkle with lime zest, and serve with the arugula.

It's ready!

Variation: Replace the butternut squash and napa cabbage with the following alternatives:

½ CUP (5½ OZ/150 G) DICED WINTER SQUASH	47
5½ OZ (150 G) SAVOY CABBAGE	39
TOTAL	491
VARIATION FOR MEN	589

NUTRITIONAL INFO

Quinoa is not a grain but a seed! It's a superfood that's high in protein (14 percent), and a source of fiber, magnesium, and iron.

SPELT
RISOTTO

Super
500

SERVES 1

PREPARATION TIME: 15 MINUTES

COOKING TIME: 35 MINUTES

INGREDIENTS	CALORIES
1 TEASPOON OLIVE OIL	45
1 GREEN ONION, CHOPPED	3
½ CUP (3 OZ/85 G) SPELT	287
2 CUPS (16 FL OZ/500 ML) HOT CHICKEN STOCK, FAT REMOVED	8
SCANT ⅔ CUP (3¼ OZ/90 G) SHELLED PEAS (8 OZ/225 G IN THEIR PODS)	72
4¼ OZ (120 G) MUSHROOMS, BRUSHED	26
2 SLICES BRESAOLA, ABOUT ½ OZ (16 G), CHOPPED (ALTERNATIVELY, USE BEEF JERKY OR OTHER DRIED MEAT)	24
1 LARGE HANDFUL (1 OZ/25 G) ARUGULA	6
1½ TEASPOONS (⅛ OZ/5 G) FRESHLY GRATED PARMESAN CHEESE	22
2 BASIL SPRIGS, LEAVES PICKED	2
TOTAL	495

VARIATION FOR MEN	
⅔ CUP (4 OZ/115 G) SPELT	388
3 CUPS (24 FL OZ/700 ML) CHICKEN STOCK, FAT REMOVED	11
TOTAL	599

Preparing my meal

Heat the olive oil in a large frying pan over medium heat, add the green onion, and sauté for 2 minutes. Add the spelt and stir so the grains are well coated. Season with salt and a little pepper and add the hot stock. Simmer over low heat, covered, for 15 minutes. Add the peas, cover, and cook for a further 10 minutes. Chop the mushrooms into pieces. Add them to the pan and cook for a further 5 minutes. Stir occasionally to obtain a creamy consistency. Serve each portion with the bresaola, arugula, a little Parmesan, and some basil leaves. Season with salt and pepper, if needed.

It's ready!

Delphine's advice: After serving the first portion, I suggest spreading out the rest of the risotto on a cold plate to stop it from cooking any further. Reheat it very gently in a saucepan with ½ cup (4 fl oz/125 ml) boiling water for a few minutes for the second portion.

Veggie version: Double the quantity of Parmesan cheese and leave out the bresaola.

TOTAL	493
VARIATION FOR MEN	597

Shopping: Spelt can easily be found in supermarkets and organic food stores.

SUMMER
SOUP

Super **500**

SERVES 1

PREPARATION TIME: 25 MINUTES

COOKING TIME: 40 MINUTES

INGREDIENTS	CALORIES
3–4 VERY FRESH RAW SCALLOPS, ABOUT 2¾ OZ (80 G)	70
1 TEASPOON CANOLA OIL	45
GRATED ZEST OF 1 ORGANIC LIME	2
3½ OZ (100 G) ASPARAGUS, CHOPPED	22
1 ZUCCHINI, ABOUT 9 OZ (250 G), DICED	42
2 CARROTS, ABOUT 7 OZ (200 G), DICED	82
½ FENNEL BULB, ABOUT 5½ OZ (150 G), DICED	47
1¾ OZ (50 G) POTATO, DICED	40
⅓ CUP (1¾ OZ/50 G) SHELLED PEAS (4½ OZ/125 G IN THEIR PODS)	40
1 BUNCH (5½ OZ/150 G) FLAT-LEAF PARSLEY	10
1 OZ (25 G) BABY SPINACH	6
1 BAY LEAF	1
2½ TABLESPOONS (1 OZ/25 G) QUINOA	92
TOTAL	499

VARIATION FOR MEN	
⅓ CUP (1¾ OZ/50 G) QUINOA	184
TOTAL	591

GLUTEN-FREE ◆

Preparing my meal

Chop the cleaned scallops into small pieces and marinate them in the fridge in the canola oil with half the lime zest and salt and pepper. Make the soup: Heat 3 cups (24 fl oz/750 ml) salted water in a medium saucepan. Add all of the vegetables (asparagus, zucchini, carrots, fennel, and potato), the shelled peas, parsley, baby spinach and bay leaf. Lightly season with pepper. Cook on a low simmer for 30 minutes. Divide into 2 meals, if you like.

First meal: Place the scallops in the bottom of a deep plate or bowl and pour a portion of hot broth and vegetables over.

Second meal: Rinse the quinoa and cook it according to the instructions on page 124. Add the quinoa to the reheated soup, sprinkle with the rest of the lime zest, and serve immediately.

It's ready!

Veggie version: Leave out the scallops and increase the quantity of quinoa. If dividing into 2 meals, split the quinoa between them.

¼ CUP (1½ OZ/40 G) QUINOA	147
TOTAL	484

VARIATION FOR MEN	
6 TABLESPOONS (2½ OZ/70 G) QUINOA	258
TOTAL	595

NUTRITIONAL INFO

Scallops are a rich source of the amino acid tryptophan, which can help to manage mood swings and assist with improving sleep.

BLACK RICE,
PEAS, ASPARAGUS & MINT

SERVES 1

PREPARATION TIME: 20 MINUTES

COOKING TIME: 1 HOUR

INGREDIENTS	CALORIES
SCANT ⅓ CUP (2 OZ/55 G) BLACK RICE	193
5½ OZ (150 G) WHITE OR GREEN ASPARAGUS	36
½ CUP (2¾ OZ/80 G) SHELLED PEAS (7 OZ/200 G IN THEIR PODS)	64
1 LARGE HANDFUL (1 OZ/25 G) ARUGULA	6
8 FRESH MINT LEAVES, CHOPPED	1
12 CHERRY TOMATOES, ABOUT 5½ OZ (150 G), CHOPPED	24
1 TEASPOON OLIVE OIL	45
1½ OZ (40 G) CANNED TUNA IN WATER, DRAINED AND FLAKED	48
1 MEDIUM EGG	71
TOTAL	488

VARIATION FOR MEN	
SCANT ½ CUP (85 G/3 OZ) BLACK RICE	298
TOTAL	593

GLUTEN-FREE ◆

Preparing my meal

Cook the back rice following the instructions on page 124. Meanwhile, peel the asparagus and cut off the woody ends. Steam the peas and the asparagus for 10 minutes. Once the rice is cooked, rinse it under cold water and drain. Let the vegetables cool, then cut the asparagus into short lengths and add it to the rice with the peas. Add the arugula and mint, the tomatoes, olive oil, and salt and pepper, and mix well. Refrigerate before eating. Divide into 2 meals, if you like.

First meal: Take a portion and add the tuna.

Second meal: Soft-boil an egg for 5–6 minutes in boiling water, then peel it under cold running water and place on top of the dish.

It's ready!

Delphine's advice: If the salad is a little dry with the tuna, add 1–2 tablespoons warm water and mix thoroughly, or purée half the tomatoes to make a little sauce.

Shopping: You'll find black rice in organic food stores.

NUTRITIONAL INFO
Black rice is a rich source of anthocyanins, an antioxidant that helps protect against the risk of cardiovascular disease, among other things.

Variation: Replace the tuna with tofy:

1½ OZ (45 G) TOFU	54
TOTAL	494
VARIATION FOR MEN	599

SCALLOPS
WITH PESTO

Super **500**

SERVES 1

PREPARATION TIME: 15 MINUTES

COOKING TIME: 20 MINUTES

INGREDIENTS	CALORIES
5–6 SCALLOPS, ABOUT 6¼ OZ (180 G)	157
GRATED ZEST AND JUICE OF 1 ORGANIC LIME	10
1¾ OZ (50 G) ZUCCHINI, CHOPPED	9
1 LARGE HANDFUL (1 OZ/25 G) ARUGULA	6
1 MINT SPRIG	1
1 TEASPOON OLIVE OIL	45
10 OZ (300 G) EDAMAME IN THEIR PODS	178
1 KALE LEAF, ABOUT ¼ OZ (10 G)	5
SCANT ½ CUP (2½ OZ/75 G) COOKED OR CANNED CHICKPEAS	84
TOTAL	**495**

VARIATION FOR MEN

6–7 SCALLOPS, ABOUT 7½ OZ (210 G)	183
12 OZ (340 G) EDAMAME IN THEIR PODS (⅞ CUP/5½ OZ/160 G SHELLED)	203
SCANT ¾ CUP (4 OZ/115 G) COOKED OR CANNED CHICKPEAS	128
TOTAL	**590**

GLUTEN-FREE ◆

Preparing my meal

Put the cleaned scallops on a small plate, sprinkle half the lime juice over, and season with salt and pepper. Cover and place in the refrigerator while making the rest of the dish. Steam the zucchini for 10 minutes. To make the pesto, purée the zucchini in a food processor with half the arugula, the remaining lime juice, half the mint leaves, the olive oil, 1 cup (8 fl oz/250 ml) water, and salt and pepper. Meanwhile, bring a saucepan of salted water to a boil and drop in the edamame for 2–3 minutes if they are frozen; 45 seconds if they have already thawed; and 8–9 minutes if they are fresh. They need to stay quite crisp. Drain and shell the beans, measure out ¾ cup (5 oz/140 g), and give the rest to your children, friends, neighbors, or pets with a dash of sweet soy sauce…delicious. Remove the thick stem of the kale and tear the leaf in half. Massage the kale by rubbing the halves together until they darken and feel silky. Cut into pieces. Rinse and drain the chickpeas and combine them with the edamame, kale, and remaining arugula leaves. Chop the rest of the mint leaves and add them to the salad with the lime zest and salt and pepper. Divide into 2 meals, if desired.

First meal: Serve half the scallops raw, especially if they are very fresh, with the salad and pesto.

Second meal: Sear the scallops in a frying pan over medium-high heat for 1 minute on each side and serve immediately with the rest of the salad and pesto.

It's ready!

Variation: You can eat all of the scallops cooked or all raw! It's up to you. Both ways are really very good.

Shopping: Edamame are a variety of soybean that is increasingly found on supermarket shelves or in the freezer section.

THAI
SALAD

SERVES 1

PREPARATION TIME: 15 MINUTES

COOKING TIME: 5 MINUTES

INGREDIENTS	CALORIES
2¼ OZ (60 G) CELLOPHANE NOODLES	199
½-INCH (1 CM) PIECE OF GINGER, GRATED	2
½ RED CHILE, SEEDED AND FINELY CHOPPED	1
1 TABLESPOON SOY SAUCE	10
½ SMALL SHALLOT, CHOPPED	3
GRATED ZEST AND JUICE OF 1 ORGANIC LIME	10
1 TEASPOON GRAPESEED OIL	45
¼ CUP (2 FL OZ/50 ML) COCONUT WATER	10
⅓ CUP (1¾ OZ/50 G) MANGO, DICED	32
2 GREEN ONIONS, THINLY SLICED	5
1½ OZ (40 G) BEAN SPROUTS	12
8 CILANTRO SPRIGS AND 2 MINT SPRIGS, CHOPPED	3
3½ OZ (100 G) COOKED SHRIMP, PEELED AND CHOPPED	80
2½ OZ (75 G) VERY FRESH RAW BLUEFIN TUNA, DICED	81
1 HANDFUL (1 OZ/25 G) BABY SALAD LEAVES	6
TOTAL	499

VARIATION FOR MEN	
2¾ OZ (80 G) CELLOPHANE NOODLES	265
3½ OZ (100 G) VERY FRESH RAW BLUEFIN TUNA, DICED	108
TOTAL	592

Preparing my meal

Put the cellophane noodles in a large bowl and pour boiling water over. Let stand for 5 minutes, then drain. Return the noodles to the bowl, cutting them up roughly with scissors. Make a dressing by combining the ginger, chile, soy sauce, shallot, lime zest and juice, grapeseed oil, and coconut water. Taste and add salt and pepper, if necessary. Pour the dressing over the noodles and mix well. Add the mango, green onions, bean sprouts, and herbs and mix together. Divide into 2 meals, if you like.

First meal: Add the shrimp chunks to one portion.

Second meal: Mix the raw tuna with the rest of the noodles. Serve each meal with a few salad leaves.

It's ready!

Tip: This dish is even better after it has marinated for a few hours in the refrigerator. Make it the day before and mix in the herbs and salad leaves just before eating.

NUTRITIONAL INFO

Shrimp are low in fat and a rich source of protein—3½ oz (100 g) shrimp contains about ¾ oz (20 g) protein and less than 1/16 oz (2 g) fat.

BULGUR
& RAW SALMON

Super
500

SERVES 1

PREPARATION TIME: 15 MINUTES

COOKING TIME: 12 MINUTES

INGREDIENTS	CALORIES
½ CUP (2½ OZ/70 G) BULGUR	240
½ TEASPOON CIDER VINEGAR	5
1 TEASPOON OLIVE OIL	45
½ SEEDLESS CUCUMBER, ABOUT 10 OZ (300 G), PEELED AND DICED	36
¼ OZ (10 G) CHIVES, SNIPPED	3
3¼ OZ (90 G) VERY FRESH RAW SALMON	150
1 SMALL BUNCH (2½ OZ/75 G) SORREL, WASHED AND COARSELY CHOPPED	19
TOTAL	498

VARIATION FOR MEN

⅔ CUP (3¼ OZ/90 G) BULGUR	309
3¾ OZ (110 G) VERY FRESH RAW SALMON	183
TOTAL	600

Preparing my meal

Cook the bulgur in two and a half times its volume of boiling salted water over medium heat, uncovered, for 7 minutes. Let stand off the heat for 5 minutes, then drain and set aside. Dress the bulgur with the vinegar and olive oil, and season with salt and pepper. Add the cucumber and chives. Set aside in the refrigerator. Clean and cut the salmon into small cubes, season with salt and pepper, and set aside in the refrigerator. At the last minute, combine the bulgur with the sorrel. Serve with the cubes of salmon on top.

It's ready!

Note: Salmon has many more calories than white fish.

Variation: Replace the salmon with raw cod and add more bulgur.

5½ OZ (150 G) VERY FRESH RAW COD	120
8½ TABLESPOONS (2¾ OZ/75 G) BULGUR	257
TOTAL	485

VARIATION FOR MEN

5½ OZ (150 G) VERY FRESH RAW COD	120
¾ CUP (3½ OZ/105 G) BULGUR	360
TOTAL	588

Variation 2: Replace the sorrel with baby spinach.

Note from Delphine: Thank you, Charlotte Lascève, for your photos but also for this fantastic recipe!

LENTIL & FISH
SALAD

SERVES 1

PREPARATION TIME: 15 MINUTES

COOKING TIME: 20 MINUTES

INGREDIENTS	CALORIES
9 TABLESPOONS (3¾ OZ/110 G) FRENCH LENTILS	387
1 GREEN ONION, THINLY SLICED	3
½ BUNCH (1½ OZ/40 G) CILANTRO, CHOPPED	5
GRATED ZEST AND JUICE OF 1 ORGANIC LEMON	12
1 TABLESPOON MUSTARD	10
1 TEASPOON OLIVE OIL	45
1½ OZ (40 G) SMOKED HADDOCK	38
TOTAL	500

VARIATION FOR MEN

3½ OZ (100 G) SMOKED HADDOCK	95
1 TABLESPOON CRÈME FRAÎCHE	30
TOTAL	587

Preparing my meal

Cook the lentils for the time indicated on the packet and let them cool (or rinse them under cold water to stop the cooking and then drain). Put the green onion, cilantro, and lemon zest and juice in a bowl, and mix together. Add the mustard and olive oil, salt lightly, season with pepper, and mix again. Add the lentils and combine. Taste and adjust the seasoning if necessary. Let the salad rest in the refrigerator before serving. Divide into 2 meals, if you like.

Second meal: As a change, add the raw smoked haddock chopped into small pieces.

Variation for men: Add the tablespoon of crème fraîche at the same time as the mustard.

It's ready!

Veggie version: Leave out the haddock and add more lentils.

10 TABLESPOONS (4¼ OZ/ 120 G) LENTILS	423
TOTAL	498

VARIATION FOR MEN	
⅔ CUP (4½ OZ/130 G) LENTILS	458
TOTAL	563

NUTRITIONAL INFO

Lentils are an excellent source of protein for vegetarians and vegans. They are a good source of iron: about 7.5 mg per 3½ oz (100 g).

FISH & VEGETABLE
CURRY

Super
500

SERVES 1

PREPARATION TIME: 25 MINUTES

COOKING TIME: 40 MINUTES

INGREDIENTS	CALORIES
½ ONION, ABOUT 1¾ OZ (50 G)	14
3½ OZ (100 G) TOMATOES	18
1 GARLIC CLOVE, CRUSHED	4
4 KAFFIR LIME LEAVES	2
¾-INCH (2-CM) PIECE OF GINGER, GRATED	3
6 CILANTRO SPRIGS	2
1 TABLESPOON SOY SAUCE	10
1 TEASPOON CURRY POWDER	6
3½ OZ (100 G) GREEN BEANS, TRIMMED	31
3½ OZ (100 G) BROCCOLI, CUT INTO FLORETS	34
¼ CUP (1¾ OZ/50 G) BROWN BASMATI RICE	174
3½ OZ (100 G) BABY SPINACH	24
3½ OZ (100 G) COD, CUT INTO PIECES	80
3½ OZ (100 G) COOKED SHRIMP, PEELED	80
½ TEASPOON BLACK SESAME SEEDS	13
TOTAL	**495**

VARIATION FOR MEN	
6 TABLESPOONS (2½ OZ/70 G) BROWN BASMATI RICE	244
4¼ OZ (120 G) COD	96
4¼ OZ (120 G) COOKED SHRIMP, PEELED	96
TOTAL	**597**

Preparing my meal

Bring 2 cups (16 fl oz/500 ml) water to a boil in a medium saucepan with the onion, tomatoes, garlic, kaffir lime leaves, ginger, cilantro stems (set aside the leaves for later), soy sauce, and curry powder. Season lightly with salt and pepper and cover. As soon as it comes to a boil, remove the lid and simmer gently for 30 minutes. Meanwhile, prepare the vegetables: steam the green beans for 15 minutes; after 8 minutes of steaming time, add the broccoli. Purée the curry sauce, making sure to remove the kaffir lime leaves first. Cook the rice following the instructions on page 90. Add the curry sauce to a deep frying pan or wok (thin out with a little boiling water if necessary). Add the green beans, broccoli, and spinach; stir and heat gently for 2 minutes. Add the fish and the shrimp, stir gently, and cook for a further 3 minutes. Serve immediately, sprinkled with chopped cilantro leaves and sesame seeds and accompanied with the rice.

It's ready!

Shopping: You can find kaffir lime leaves in well-stocked supermarkets or Asian food stores, often in the freezer section. You can replace them with 1 lemongrass stalk. Remove the outer layer of the lemongrass stalk and trim the base. Cut the more tender part into short lengths, stopping as soon as it becomes woody.

Tip: Feel free to double the quantities on Non-Fast Days for a family meal or dinner with friends. In this case, slightly increase the amount of rice and add ½ cup (4 fl oz/125 ml) coconut milk to the sauce.

NUTRITIONAL INFO
Sesame seeds are another superfood, a rich source of omega-3 fatty acids.

FISH & BEAN SALAD,
COLD OR HOT!

Super
500

SERVES 1

PREPARATION TIME: 15 MINUTES

COOKING TIME: 10 MINUTES

INGREDIENTS	CALORIES
SCANT 1 CUP (5 OZ/140 G) COOKED OR CANNED KIDNEY BEANS (SEE NOTE)	178
½ CUP (3¼ OZ/90 G) COOKED OR CANNED CHICKPEAS (SEE NOTE)	100
1 SMALL FENNEL BULB, ABOUT 5½ OZ (150 G)	47
2 GREEN ONIONS	5
1 LARGE HANDFUL (1 OZ/25 G) ARUGULA, CHOPPED	6
12 CHERRY TOMATOES, ABOUT 5½ OZ (150 G), CHOPPED	24
2 FLAT-LEAF PARSLEY SPRIGS, CHOPPED	1
2 TARRAGON SPRIGS, CHOPPED	1
1 TEASPOON HAZELNUT OIL	45
2¾ OZ (80 G) COD FILLET OR OTHER FIRM WHITE FISH	64
TOTAL	471

VARIATION FOR MEN	
1 LARGE EGG	90
TOTAL	561

GLUTEN-FREE ◆

Preparing my meal

Rinse the kidney beans and chickpeas and put them in a bowl. Discard the hard outer layer of the fennel and thinly slice the fennel and green onions. Add the fennel and onions, the arugula, tomatoes, and herbs to the beans and chickpeas. Dress with the hazelnut oil and salt and pepper. Divide into 2 meals, if desired.

First meal: Steam the piece of fish for 6 minutes, let cool, and gently combine with a portion of salad.

Second meal: Add 3 tablespoons water to the salad and warm gently in a saucepan to eat hot.

Variation for men: Soft-boil an egg for 5–6 minutes in boiling water, then peel it under cold running water and add to the hot version for dinner.

It's ready!

Tip: This salad is very hearty and nutritious; it is ideal for the early days of fasting. You can choose whether to eat the fish at lunch or dinnertime.

Shopping: Use canned kidney beans and chickpeas! There are some very good products available. Be sure to look for plain beans without sauce, and buy low-sodium and organic versions when available. To use dried beans and chickpeas, follow the instructions on the packets to cook the beans and chickpeas before using, or refer to the recipe for kidney beans on page 124.

Veggie version: Leave out the fish and add more kidney beans.

HEAPING 1 CUP (6¼ OZ/180 G) COOKED OR CANNED BEANS	229
TOTAL	458
VARIATION FOR MEN TOTAL	548

PASTA
SALAD

Super
500

SERVES 1

PREPARATION TIME: 15 MINUTES

COOKING TIME: 10 MINUTES

INGREDIENTS	CALORIES
3½ OZ (100 G) PASTA (OF YOUR CHOICE)	345
8 CHERRY TOMATOES, ABOUT 3½ OZ (100 G)	18
1 TEASPOON OLIVE OIL	45
½ GARLIC CLOVE	2
ZEST AND JUICE OF ½ ORGANIC LIME	5
1 LARGE HANDFUL (1 OZ/25 G) ARUGULA, COARSELY CHOPPED	6
½ ZUCCHINI, ABOUT 4½ OZ (125 G), DICED	21
¼ CUP (1 OZ/30 G) CAPERBERRIES	8
3 BASIL SPRIGS, LEAVES PICKED	3
1¼ OZ (35 G) CANNED TUNA IN WATER, DRAINED AND FLAKED	41
TOTAL	**494**

VARIATION FOR MEN

4¼ OZ (120 G) PASTA (OF YOUR CHOICE)	414
2¼ OZ (60 G) CANNED TUNA IN WATER, DRAINED AND FLAKED	69
TOTAL	**591**

Preparing my meal

Cook the pasta until al dente following the packet instructions. Run it immediately under cold water to stop the cooking, then drain. Purée half the tomatoes in a food processor with the olive oil, 2 tablespoons water, the garlic, salt, pepper, and lime juice. Pour the sauce over the pasta and toss. Add the arugula, the rest of the tomatoes (chopped), the zucchini, caperberries, lime zest, and basil leaves. Mix again.

Second meal: Add the tuna and mix it in.

It's ready!

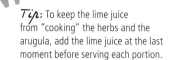

Tip: To keep the lime juice from "cooking" the herbs and the arugula, add the lime juice at the last moment before serving each portion.

Shopping: If you can't find caperberries, use the smaller capers sold in jars.

Veggie version: Leave out the tuna and add more pasta.

3¾ OZ (110 G) PASTA	380
TOTAL	**488**

VARIATION FOR MEN

5 OZ (140 G) PASTA	483
TOTAL	**591**

NUTRITIONAL INFO

Consider using whole-grain or semi–whole grain pasta. It doesn't affect the number of calories but it's more healthy: it has more fiber, vitamins, and minerals.

CHICKEN, ENDIVE,
LETTUCE &
ARTICHOKES

Super
500

SERVES 1

PREPARATION TIME: 25 MINUTES

MARINATING TIME: 30 MINUTES

COOKING TIME: 11 MINUTES

INGREDIENTS	CALORIES
JUICE OF ½ ORANGE, ABOUT ¼ CUP (2 FL OZ/50 ML)	23
1 TEASPOON OLIVE OIL	45
1 SCANT TEASPOON AGAVE SYRUP	16
6¼ OZ (180 G) BONELESS, SKINLESS CHICKEN BREAST	216
2 TABLESPOONS (¾ OZ/20 G) COUSCOUS	75
5½ OZ (150 G) BELGIAN ENDIVE	26
1 LITTLE GEM OR BABY ROMAINE LETTUCE HEART	8
2 GREEN ONONS	5
4 COOKED ARTICHOKE HEARTS, ABOUT 3½ OZ (100 G), CHOPPED INTO SMALL PIECES	34
2 TARRAGON SPRIGS	2
1 TEASPOON HEMP SEEDS	33
GRATED ZEST OF ½ ORGANIC ORANGE	2
TOTAL	485

VARIATION FOR MEN

8¼ OZ (230 G) BONELESS, SKINLESS CHICKEN BREAST	276
2½ TABLESPOONS (1 OZ/30 G) COUSCOUS	112
TOTAL	582

Preparing my meal

Make a marinade from the orange juice, olive oil, agave syrup, and a little salt and pepper. Cut the chicken breast in half horizontally and marinate it in the refrigerator for 30 minutes. Make the couscous as indicated on the packet, omitting any oil or butter and being careful not to overcook it. Once it is cooked, fluff it up with a fork and set aside. Slice the endive and lettuce into strips. Slice the green onions. Drain the chicken breast, reserving the marinade. Sear the chicken in a hot frying pan for 2 minutes on each side: it should be lightly browned. Slice the chicken into strips and set aside. In the same frying pan, brown half the endive, lettuce, and green onions for 5 minutes over high heat, stirring occasionally. Add the artichoke hearts, tarragon, chicken, marinade, and couscous; mix together and cook for a further 2 minutes, making sure the marinade comes to a boil. Transfer everything from the frying pan to a mixing bowl and add the rest of the vegetables. Mix together and serve sprinkled with hemp seeds and orange zest.

Second meal: Warm gently in the pan. (Alternatively, it's also very good served cold.)

It's ready!

Veggie version: Leave out the chicken, add tofu, and increase the quantity of couscous.

1¾ OZ (50 G) SMOKED TOFU, DICED	60
⅓ CUP (2¼ OZ/60 G) COUSCOUS	225
TOTAL	479

VARIATION FOR MEN

1¾ OZ (50 G) SMOKED TOFU	60
½ CUP (3¼ OZ/90 G) COUSCOUS	336
TOTAL	590

Shopping: You can find hemp seeds in organic supermarkets. You can replace them with 1 teaspoon sesame seeds (26 calories).

CHICKEN STIR-FRY
WITH BEAN SPROUTS

Super
500

SERVES 1
PREPARATION TIME: 20 MINUTES
COOKING TIME: 25 MINUTES

INGREDIENTS	CALORIES
⅓ CUP (2¼ OZ/60 G) BULGUR	206
5½ OZ (150 G) NAPA CABBAGE	18
3½ OZ (100 G) BONELESS, SKINLESS CHICKEN BREAST	120
1 TEASPOON OLIVE OIL	45
½-INCH (1-CM) PIECE OF GINGER, GRATED	2
1 SMALL SHALLOT, CHOPPED	7
1 GREEN ONION, THINLY SLICED	3
½ GARLIC CLOVE, CRUSHED	2
9 OZ (250 G) BEAN SPROUTS	75
2 TABLESPOONS COCONUT WATER	5
1 TEASPOON SOY SAUCE	5
8 CILANTRO SPRIGS, CHOPPED	3
½ LIME, CUT INTO WEDGES	4
TOTAL	495

VARIATION FOR MEN	
9 TABLESPOONS (2¾ OZ/80 G) BULGUR	274
4½ OZ (130 G) BONELESS, SKINLESS CHICKEN BREAST	156
TOTAL	599

Preparing my meal

Cook the bulgur in two and a half times its volume of boiling salted water, over medium heat, uncovered, for 7 minutes. Let stand off the heat for 5 minutes, then drain and set aside. Slice the cabbage leaves into fairly wide strips. Cut the chicken breast into small pieces. Add the olive oil to a hot wok over high heat, then sauté the chicken pieces with the ginger, shallot, and green onion until well browned on all sides, about 2 minutes. Add the garlic, cabbage, half the bean sprouts, and ¼ cup (2 fl oz/50 ml) water. Continue cooking over medium heat for 8 minutes, stirring often. Once cooked, add the coconut water and soy sauce. Season lightly with salt and well with pepper, and mix together. Serve alongside the warmed bulgur with the chopped cilantro sprinkled on top. Add as many of the rest of the bean sprouts as you like, and serve with wedges of lime.

It's ready!

Seafood version: Replace the chicken with peeled raw shrimp. For these quantities the calories are the same.

5½ OZ (150 G) SHIRMP	120
VARIATION FOR MEN	
6¾ OZ (195 G) SHRIMP	156

Tip: Scale up the quantities and this dish makes an ideal family meal for a Non-Fast Day!

NUTRITIONAL INFO

Bean sprouts are a good source of folate, essential for the synthesis of DNA and production of red blood cells.

VEAL
WITH PRESERVED LEMON

SERVES 1

PREPARATION TIME: 10 MINUTES

MARINATING TIME: 1 HOUR

COOKING TIME: 3 HOURS

INGREDIENTS	CALORIES
½ PRESERVED LEMON	9
½ GARLIC CLOVE, CRUSHED	2
½ ONION, ABOUT 1¾ OZ (50 G), SLICED	14
8 CHERRY TOMATOES, ABOUT 3½ OZ (100 G), QUARTERED	18
2 LARGE HANDFULS (1 OZ/30 G) CILANTRO LEAVES, CHOPPED	4
JUICE OF 1 LEMON	10
1 TEASPOON OLIVE OIL	45
3½ OZ (100 G) VEAL TENDERLOIN, CUT INTO PIECES	140
⅓ CUP (1¾ OZ/50 G) SHELLED PEAS (4½ OZ/125 G IN THEIR PODS)	40
⅓ CUP (1¾ OZ/50 G) COOKED ARTICHOKE HEARTS, CHOPPED	17
⅓ CUP (2 OZ/55 G) SPELT COUSCOUS	188
1¾ OZ (50 G) BABY SPINACH, WASHED	12
TOTAL	499

VARIATION FOR MEN	
4¼ OZ (120 G) VEAL TENDERLOIN, CUT INTO PIECES	168
SCANT ½ CUP (2½ OZ/75 G) SPELT COUSCOUS	257
TOTAL	596

Preparing my meal

Rinse the preserved lemon under cold running water and remove the seeds, then slice. In a small flameproof casserole dish, combine the garlic, onion, preserved lemon, tomatoes, half the cilantro, the lemon juice, olive oil, and pepper. Be careful not to add salt to this dish, as the preserved lemon already provides salt. Add the pieces of veal to this marinade, stir, and marinate for 1 hour in the refrigerator. Preheat the oven to 300°F (150°C). Cover the meat with water, bring to a boil on the stove top, then cover the casserole dish and bake in the oven for at least 3 hours. Check the dish occasionally, adding a little water if necessary. Fifteen minutes before the end of the cooking time, add the peas and the artichoke hearts. Cook the couscous in three times its volume of boiling salted water for 8 minutes over medium heat, then let it stand off the heat for 5 minutes. Serve the veal accompanied with the couscous, baby spinach, and the rest of the cilantro.

It's ready!

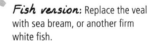

Fish version: Replace the veal with sea bream, or another firm white fish.

5 OZ (140 G) SEA BREAM FILLET	140
TOTAL	499

VARIATION FOR MEN	
5¾ OZ (165 G) SEA BREAM FILLET	165
TOTAL	593

Method: Cook the marinade in the casserole dish with 1 cup (8 fl oz/ 250 ml) of water in the oven for 1 hour. Add the vegetables and fish (cut into chunks) and cook for another 15 minutes. It's simple, fast, and amazingly good.

Tip: This dish is also very good for Non-Fast Days. Increase the amount of meat a little and add other vegetables (carrots, turnips, etc.).

NUTRITIONAL INFO

Spelt is a very nutritious whole grain, perfect for Fast Days! It is a species of wheat, but since it has a lower gluten content than ordinary wheat, it can sometimes be tolerated by people who are sensitive to gluten.

LIKE A CHILI

SERVES 1

PREPARATION TIME: 15 MINUTES

COOKING TIME: 35 MINUTES

+ 45 MINUTES FOR RICE (MEN'S VERSION)

INGREDIENTS	CALORIES
1 TEASPOON OLIVE OIL	45
½ RED ONION, CHOPPED	15
1 PINCH GROUND CUMIN	1
1¾ OZ (50 G) GROUND BEEF, 95% LEAN	64
5½ OZ (150 G) TOMATOES	24
1 TEASPOON CHOPPED OREGANO	1
1¾ OZ (50 G) BABY SPINACH, CHOPPED	12
1 PINCH CAYENNE PEPPER	1
1 GARLIC CLOVE, CHOPPED	4
1½ CUPS (9 OZ/255 G) COOKED OR CANNED KIDNEY BEANS (SEE NOTE)	324
3 FLAT-LEAF PARSLEY SPRIGS, CHOPPED	2
TOTAL	493

VARIATION FOR MEN

2½ TABLESPOONS (1 OZ/30 G) BROWN RICE	104
TOTAL	597

GLUTEN-FREE ◆

Preparing my meal

Heat the olive oil in a small flameproof casserole dish over medium heat. Add the onion and cumin and cook for 5 minutes. Raise the heat, add the meat, and brown, breaking it up with a fork. Be careful not to let it stew—the dish needs to be very hot so that the meat sears. Add 4 fl oz (120 ml) water, the tomatoes, oregano, half the baby spinach, the cayenne, garlic, and salt and pepper. Let it cook on a low simmer for 15 minutes. Rinse and add the beans and the parsley, cover, and simmer for 10 minutes. At serving time, add the rest of the spinach and combine.

Variation for men: Serve with brown rice. Fill a pot with water, add the rice and a pinch of salt, bring to a boil, and cook over medium-high heat, uncovered, for 30 minutes. Drain, return to the pot, cover, and let steam for 10 minutes before serving.

It's ready!

Note from Delphine: My daughter Maé adores chili. I double the quantities and we're set. I'm not all alone with my "Super 500," and I make her happy.

Veggie version: Leave out the ground beef and add (or increase for men's variation) the brown rice.

2 SCANT TABLESPOONS (¾ OZ/20 G) BROWN RICE	69
TOTAL	498

VARIATION FOR MEN

¼ CUP (1½ OZ/45 G) BROWN RICE	156
TOTAL	585

Home-cooked beans: Follow the instructions on page 124 to cook dried beans before using.

NUTRITIONAL INFO

Can you eat spicy foods like chiles to lose weight? Some studies have found that capsaicin, a compound found in chiles, increases the feeling of fullness and stimulates the metabolism.

THAI VEGETABLE
SOUP

Super
500

SERVES 1

PREPARATION TIME: 25 MINUTES

COOKING TIME: 35 MINUTES

INGREDIENTS	CALORIES
3½ OZ (100 G) THAI EGGPLANT	24
3½ OZ (100 G) MUSHROOMS	22
3½ OZ (100 G) GREEN BEANS	31
1 LEMONGRASS STALK	2
3½ OZ (100 G) BONELESS, SKINLESS CHICKEN BREAST	120
¾-INCH (2-CM) PIECE OF GINGER, GRATED	4
½ GARLIC CLOVE, CRUSHED	2
3 CUPS (24 FL OZ/750 ML) CHICKEN STOCK, FAT REMOVED	12
1 TEASPOON RED CURRY PASTE	7
JUICE OF 1 LIME	8
4 KAFFIR LIME LEAVES	2
½ BUNCH (1½ OZ/40 G) CILANTRO, CHOPPED	5
8 CHERRY TOMATOES, ABOUT 3½ OZ (100 G)	18
2 OZ (55 G) CELLOPHANE NOODLES	183
1¾ OZ (50 G) BEAN SPROUTS	15
1 TEASPOON SESAME OIL	45
TOTAL	500

VARIATION FOR MEN	
5 OZ (140 G) BONELESS, SKINLESS CHICKEN BREAST	168
2½ OZ (70 G) CELLOPHANE NOODLES	233
TOTAL	598

Preparing my meal

Prepare all the vegetables: quarter the eggplant, brush and chop the mushrooms into pieces, and cut the green beans into long sections. Remove the outer layer of the lemongrass stalk, trim the base, and cut into short lengths. Cut the chicken breast into cubes. Heat a nonstick frying pan over high heat and brown the chicken for 5 minutes with the ginger and garlic. Be careful not to let it burn, reducing the heat if necessary. Keep the chicken warm. Heat the chicken stock with the red curry paste, lime juice, kaffir lime leaves, and lemongrass, and bring to a boil. Add the eggplant, chicken, green beans, and half the cilantro. Reduce the heat and simmer for 20 minutes. Before serving, add the mushrooms, tomatoes, noodles, and bean sprouts, and cook for another 5 minutes. Dress with a little sesame oil and scatter the rest of the cilantro over before serving.

It's ready!

Veggie version: Leave out the chicken and increase the quantity of noodles.

3¼ OZ (90 G) CELLOPHANE NOODLES	299
TOTAL	496

VARIATION FOR MEN	
4¼ OZ (120 G) CELLOPHANE NOODLES	399
TOTAL	596

Delphine's advice: If dividing into 2 meals, I suggest setting aside half the tomatoes, noodles, and bean sprouts for the second meal, and cooking them when reheating the soup.

Shopping: If you go to an Asian food store, buy a few leaves of Thai basil, whose aroma and flavor will work beautifully with this delicious soup. If you can't find Thai eggplant, use 3½ oz (100 g) of regular eggplant, cut into large cubes.

Kaffir lime leaves are sold in well-stocked supermarkets and Asian stores, sometimes in the freezer section. Replace the lime leaves with an extra lemongrass stalk if you can't get them.

BEEF & CARROTS

Super **500**

SERVES 1

PREPARATION TIME: 10 MINUTES

COOKING TIME: 3 HOURS

INGREDIENTS	CALORIES
3½ OZ (100 G) BEEF ROUND OR SIRLOIN STEAK, CUT INTO PIECES	160
9 OZ (250 G) CARROTS, CUT INTO LARGE PIECES	103
2 SMALL SHALLOTS	15
GRATED ZEST OF ½ ORGANIC ORANGE	2
½ TEASPOON FENNEL SEEDS	3
⅓ CUP (2¼ OZ/60 G) BROWN BASMATI RICE	207
2 FLAT-LEAF PARSLEY SPRIGS, CHOPPED	2
1 LARGE HANDFUL (1 OZ/25 G) ARUGULA	6
TOTAL	498

VARIATION FOR MEN

5 OZ (140 G) BEEF ROUND OR SIRLOIN STEAK, CUT INTO PIECES	224
6 TABLESPOONS (2½ OZ/70 G) BROWN BASMATI RICE	244
TOTAL	599

GLUTEN-FREE ◆

Preparing my meal

Preheat the oven to 300°F (150°C). Put the meat in a small flameproof casserole dish with the carrots, shallots, orange zest, fennel seeds, and salt and pepper. Cover the meat with water and bring to a boil on the stove top, then cover and bake in the oven for at least 3 hours. Cook the rice in a pot of boiling salted water, uncovered, for 11 minutes over medium heat. Drain, return to the pot, cover, and let steam for a few minutes. Serve the beef and carrots sprinkled with parsley and accompanied with the rice, broth, and arugula.

It's ready!

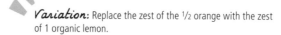

Variation: Replace the zest of the ½ orange with the zest of 1 organic lemon.

Tip: This dish is also very good for Non-Fast Days—or non-fasters. Add some roasting potatoes and slightly increase the amount of meat.

Note from Delphine: Oops! Some friends ask themselves over to dinner on a day I want to be a Fast Day. No problem! I double or triple the quantities and make sure that I don't take more than my share.

NUTRITIONAL INFO

Beef is an excellent source of vitamin B and zinc, which play a role in maintaining a healthy immune system. Lean beef is surprisingly low in fat. You can take advantage of it on your Fast Days!

RED RICE
WITH CAULIFLOWER & SPROUTS

Super
500

SERVES 1
PREPARATION TIME: 20 MINUTES
COOKING TIME: 45 MINUTES

INGREDIENTS	CALORIES
6 TABLESPOONS (2¾ OZ/80 G) RED RICE	290
1¾ OZ (50 G) BONELESS, SKINLESS CHICKEN BREAST	60
3½ OZ (100 G) CAULIFLOWER	25
JUICE OF 1 LEMON, ABOUT 1½ TABLESPOONS (¾ FL OZ/25 ML)	10
1 TEASPOON OLIVE OIL	45
1 TEASPOON CANOLA OIL	45
1¾ OZ (50 G) SPROUTS (SUCH AS CABBAGE OR ALFALFA)	14
2 GREEN ONIONS, THINLY SLICED	5
4 MINT SPRIGS AND 4 PARSLEY SPRIGS, CHOPPED	4
TOTAL	498

VARIATION FOR MEN	
½ CUP (3½ OZ/105 G) RED RICE	381
TOTAL	589

GLUTEN-FREE ♦

Preparing my meal

Pour the rice into a medium saucepan with three times its volume of cold water. Add salt and cook for 45 minutes on a low simmer. Let the rice cool or stop it from cooking any further by rinsing it under cold water, then drain. Meanwhile, steam the chicken for 10 minutes. Let it cool and cut into small cubes. Prepare the cauliflower: Using a mandoline, shred the top of the florets to make a "cauliflower rice." In a bowl, combine the lemon juice with the oils and two or three turns of the pepper mill. Add the chicken, the cauliflower rice, the sprouts, green onions, and herbs. Mix well and place in the refrigerator. When serving, taste and adjust the salt and pepper if necessary.

It's ready!

 Tip: To stop the lemon juice from "cooking" the herbs, add them at the last minute.

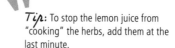 *Shopping:* You'll find red rice in organic food stores.

Veggie version:
Leave out the chicken and increase the quantity of red rice.

½ CUP (3¼ OZ/95 G) RED RICE	344
TOTAL	492

VARIATION FOR MEN	
9 TABLESPOONS (4¼ OZ/ 120 G) RED RICE	435
TOTAL	583

NUTRITIONAL INFO
Cauliflower, a member of the Brassicaceae family, is a real superfood. This family of vegetables contains phytonutrients called glucosinolates, which help optimize liver function and support the body's natural detoxification cycles.

CHARLOTTE'S
PILAF

Super
500

SERVES 1
PREPARATION TIME: 15 MINUTES
COOKING TIME: 1 HOUR

INGREDIENTS	CALORIES
½ RED ONION	15
3½ OZ (100 G) FENNEL BULB	31
½ RED BELL PEPPER, ABOUT 4½ OZ (125 G)	31
⅔ CUP (2¾ OZ/80 G) CUBED BUTTERNUT SQUASH	40
1 TEASPOON OLIVE OIL	45
1 SMALL CHICKEN THIGH, ABOUT 3½ OZ (100 G)	95
1 GARLIC CLOVE	4
¼ CUP (1¾ OZ/50 G) MILLET	189
1 TEASPOON BALSAMIC VINEGAR	2
2 BASIL SPRIGS, CHOPPED	2
4 CHIVES, SNIPPED	1
2 LARGE HANDFULS (1¾ OZ/50 G) SPINACH OR ARUGULA	12
1½ TEASPOONS (⅛ OZ/5 G) FRESHLY GRATED PARMESAN CHEESE	22
TOTAL	489

VARIATION FOR MEN

⅓ CUP (2½ OZ/70 G) MILLET	265
1 TABLESPOON (¼ OZ/10 G) FRESHLY GRATED PARMESAN CHEESE	44
TOTAL	587

GLUTEN-FREE ◆

Preparing my meal

Preheat the oven to 400°F (200°C). Cut the onion into cubes. Discard the hard outer layer of the fennel bulb, then cut the fennel and the the bell pepper into pieces. Put all the vegetables in a baking dish, add 2 drops of the olive oil and salt and pepper, stir together, and cook in the oven for 15 minutes, stirring occasionally. Add the chicken thigh and garlic, and cook for another 45 minutes. Meanwhile, put the millet in a medium saucepan with a large quantity of salted water, and cook for 15 minutes. Run the millet under cold water to stop the cooking and drain. Remove the garlic from the baking dish, peel, and crush. Make a vinaigrette by mixing the garlic with the rest of the olive oil, the balsamic vinegar, salt and pepper, and 1 teaspoon of water. Pull the chicken thigh apart to remove the skin, fat, and bones, and cut the flesh into small pieces. Combine the millet with the vegetables and herbs. Dress the salad with the vinaigrette. Divide into 2 meals, if desired.

First meal: Add the chicken and half the salad.

Second meal: Add the grated Parmesan and the other half of the salad.

It's ready!

Variation: Replace the millet with brown basmati rice. See page 90 for cooking instructions.

¼ CUP (1¾ OZ/50 G) BROWN BASMATI RICE	175
TOTAL	475

VARIATION FOR MEN

6 TABLESPOONS (2½ OZ/75 G) BROWN BASMATI RICE	262
TOTAL	584

NUTRITIONAL INFO

Millet is not just for the birds. This little seed is high in protein and magnesium, with a taste that's similar to that of hazelnut.

Note from Delphine: Thanks to Charlotte "the redhead" for this delicious recipe, original and complete!

Chapter 2

À LA CARTE RECIPES

CRISPY
BELGIAN ENDIVE

103 *calories*

SERVES 1

PREPARATION TIME: 10 MINUTES

COOKING TIME: 10 MINUTES

INGREDIENTS	CALORIES
2 BELGIAN ENDIVES, ABOUT 7 OZ (200 G)	34
2 BASIL SPRIGS	2
1 FLAT-LEAF PARSLEY SPRIG	1
2 TABLESPOONS LEMON JUICE	6
1 SCANT TEASPOON AGAVE SYRUP	16
1 TABLESPOON (¼ OZ/10 G) FRESHLY GRATED PARMESAN CHEESE	44
TOTAL	103

GLUTEN-FREE ♦

Preparing my meal

Cut the endives in half lengthwise. Tear the basil and pluck the parsley leaves from the stems, and slip the herbs between the endive leaves. Heat the broiler. Put the endives in a baking dish and sprinkle with the lemon juice, agave syrup, half the Parmesan cheese, and salt and pepper. Slide under the broiler (not too close) and cook for 10 minutes to make them nice and crispy. Make sure they don't burn—move them away from the broiler or put some foil on top as soon as they are golden brown. Serve with the remaining Parmesan cheese.

It's ready!

Extra: For a more complete meal, serve with grilled meat or steamed pollack or cod.

MEAT	
3½ OZ (100 G) GRILLED STEAK	136
TOTAL	239
FISH	
4¼ OZ (120 G) POLLACK	108
TOTAL	211

TOMATO TART

197 *calories*

SERVES 1

PREPARATION TIME: 15 MINUTES

COOKING TIME: 10 MINUTES

INGREDIENTS	CALORIES
1½ OZ (40 G) PUFF PASTRY, CUT FROM SHEET OF PASTRY (SEE METHOD)	152
16 CHERRY TOMATOES, ABOUT 7 OZ (200 G)	36
½ TEASPOON MUSTARD	3
½ TEASPOON TOMATO PASTE	5
1 BASIL SPRIG	1
TOTAL	197

Preparing my meal

Preheat the oven to 400°F (200°C). Cut a 5½-inch (14-cm) round from a sheet of puff pastry and reserve the rest of the pastry for another use. Place the pastry base on some parchment paper, prick with a fork, and place in the refrigerator. Wash the tomatoes and slice them into thin rounds. Mix together the mustard and tomato paste. Retrieve the pastry base from the refrigerator and spread the mustard-tomato mixture over the base, then arrange the tomato slices arranged on top. Season with salt and pepper and cook for 10 minutes in the middle of the oven. At serving time, scatter the basil leaves over.

It's ready!

Note: Choose the lightest possible pastry (the calories will be shown on the packet). Don't go above 400 calories per 3½ oz (100 g) of pastry.

Variation: You can top the tart with arugula.

1 LARGE HANDFUL (1 OZ/25 G) ARUGULA	6
TOTAL	203

CRISP
& TANGY SALAD

87 *calories*

SERVES 1

PREPARATION TIME: 10 MINUTES

INGREDIENTS	CALORIES
3 LITTLE GEM OR BABY ROMAINE LETTUCES	23
1 BASIL SPRIG	1
⅓ PRESERVED LEMON	7
⅓ TEASPOON GROUND CUMIN	2
4 CHERRY TOMATOES, ABOUT 1¾ OZ (50 G)	9
1 TEASPOON OLIVE OIL	45
TOTAL	87

GLUTEN-FREE ◆

Preparing my meal

Chop the lettuce leaves into bite-sized pieces. Pick the basil leaves and set aside. Rinse the preserved lemon under cold running water and remove the seeds. Combine the preserved lemon, cumin, tomatoes, olive oil, and pepper in the bowl of a food processor. Purée together and pour over the salad. Add the basil leaves, toss, and serve.

It's ready!

Extra: Add some chicken breast, steamed for 10 minutes and thinly sliced, or some cooked shrimp.

CHICKEN	
4½ OZ (120 G) BONELESS, SKINLESS CHICKEN BREAST	144
TOTAL	231

SHRIMP	
3½ OZ (100 G) COOKED SHRIMP	80
TOTAL	167

FRUITY
GRATED CARROTS

86 *calories*

SERVES 1

PREPARATION TIME: 10 MINUTES

INGREDIENTS	CALORIES
5½ OZ (150 G) CARROTS	62
1 TEASPOON LEMON JUICE	2
1 TABLESPOON FRESHLY SQUEEZED ORANGE JUICE	2
1 SCANT TEASPOON AGAVE SYRUP	16
1 TEASPOON WHITE WINE VINEGAR	2
5 CILANTRO SPRIGS, LEAVES CHOPPED	2
TOTAL	**86**

GLUTEN-FREE ◆

Preparing my meal

Shred the carrots on the largest holes of a box grater. Make a vinaigrette by combining the lemon juice, orange juice, agave syrup, vinegar, and salt and pepper, and mix it with the carrots. Let the salad stand for at least 1 hour in the refrigerator before eating; it will be tastier and juicier. At the last minute, scatter the cilantro over.

Sweet and sour variation: Add grated mango to the mixture.

⅓ CUP (1¾ OZ/50 G) MANGO	32
TOTAL	**118**

Nutty variation: Add toasted and crushed hazelnuts to the salad at the last minute.

WITHOUT MANGO

1 HEAPING TABLESPOON (¼ OZ/10 G) HAZELNUTS	63
TOTAL	**149**

WITH MANGO

TOTAL	**181**

SPRING
ASPARAGUS

85 *calories*

SERVES 1

PREPARATION TIME: 15 MINUTES

COOKING TIME: 15 MINUTES

INGREDIENTS	CALORIES
5½ OZ (150 G) WHITE OR GREEN ASPARAGUS	36
1 TEASPOON LEMON JUICE	2
1 TEASPOON OLIVE OIL	45
FLEUR DE SEL (FINE SEA SALT)	
10 CHIVES, SNIPPED	2
TOTAL	85

GLUTEN-FREE ◆

Preparing my meal

Trim the bases of the asparagus spears, then peel them without touching the tip—this would be a sacrilege because it's the best part! Rinse them under cold water and steam for 10–15 minutes, depending on their size. Make a vinaigrette by mixing the lemon juice, olive oil, 1 teaspoon water, sea salt, and pepper. Check whether the asparagus spears are cooked by inserting the tip of a knife into one of the spears. Let them cool until just warm and serve, sprinkled with chives and accompanied with the vinaigrette.

It's ready!

Tip: You can also poach the asparagus in simmering water. Tie the bunch together with string so the asparagus doesn't roam around and get damaged.

Extra: Add some freshly grated Parmesan cheese. Use a Microplane grater to create very light grated cheese.

1½ TEASPOONS (⅛ OZ/5 G) PARMESAN CHEESE	22
TOTAL	107

Extra: Serve with cod or other firm white fish, steamed for 10 minutes, and some quinoa. (See page 124 for quinoa cooking instructions.)

3½ OZ (100 G) COD	80
¼ CUP (1½ OZ/40 G) UNCOOKED QUINOA	147
TOTAL	312

STEAMED
HEIRLOOM VEGETABLES

117 *calories*

SERVES 1

PREPARATION TIME: 15 MINUTES

COOKING TIME: 20 MINUTES

INGREDIENTS	CALORIES
1¾ OZ (50 G) JERUSALEM ARTICHOKES	37
1¾ OZ (50 G) TURNIP (COLORED ONES ARE PRETTIER)	15
1¾ OZ (50 G) BLACK RADISH (ALTERNATIVELY, USE RUTABAGA)	10
1¾ OZ (50 G) PARSNIP	38
¾ OZ (20 G) RAW BEETS	5
½ TEASPOON CHIA SEEDS	10
5 CHERVIL SPRIGS, CHOPPED	2
TOTAL	117

GLUTEN-FREE ◆

Preparing my meal

Peel and cut the Jerusalem artichokes, turnip, black radish, and parsnip into similar-sized pieces. Steam them for 20 minutes. As soon as they are cooked, transfer them to a plate. Grate the beet over the top, salt lightly and season with pepper, sprinkle with chia seeds, and scatter the chervil over.

It's ready!

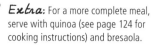

Extra: For a more complete meal, serve with quinoa (see page 124 for cooking instructions) and bresaola.

3½ TABLESPOONS (1¼ OZ/ 35 G) UNCOOKED QUINOA	128
3 SLICES (1 OZ/24 G) BRESAOLA (ALTERNATIVELY, USE BEEF JERKY OR OTHER DRIED MEAT)	36
TOTAL	281

Tip: If you choose organic vegetables, you won't need to peel the radish, turnip, and parsnip after rinsing them under water.

NUTRITIONAL INFO

Chia seeds are very good for you and are part of the family of foods rich in omega-3 fatty acids. You'll find them in organic food shops.

BOWL OF PASTA

324 *calories*

SERVES 1

PREPARATION TIME: 15 MINUTES

COOKING TIME: 10 MINUTES

INGREDIENTS	CALORIES
2½ OZ (75 G) WHOLE-WHEAT PASTA	258
3½ OZ (100 G) TOMATOES	18
5 ARUGULA LEAVES	2
½ TEASPOON OLIVE OIL	23
1 BASIL SPRIG, LEAVES PICKED	1
1½ TEASPOONS (⅛ OZ/5 G) FRESHLY GRATED PARMESAN CHEESE	22
TOTAL	324

Preparing my meal

Cook the pasta until al dente following the packet instructions (to keep its glycemic index lower—the more pasta is cooked, the faster its carbohydrates are released!). Purée the tomatoes in a blender with the arugula, olive oil, and a little salt and pepper. Heat this sauce for a few minutes in a saucepan over medium heat and pour it over the pasta as soon as it is cooked. Scatter the basil leaves and Parmesan over.

It's ready!

Note from Delphine: Like the tomato tart, this recipe "costs" a lot of calories for its serving size! But it's good to give yourself a "different" kind of indulgence from time to time.

Extra: Add some canned tuna in water or cooked ground beef to the sauce when heating it up.

TUNA

1 OZ (25 G) TUNA IN WATER, DRAINED	29
TOTAL	353

BEEF

1 OZ (25 G) GROUND BEEF (95% LEAN)	34
TOTAL	358

STEAMED BROCCOLI
& SOY SAUCE

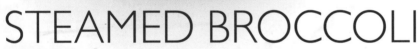

66 calories

SERVES 1
PREPARATION TIME: 5 MINUTES
COOKING TIME: 7 MINUTES

INGREDIENTS	CALORIES
4½ OZ (130 G) BROCCOLI FLORETS	44
1 TABLESPOON RICE VINEGAR	4
1 TEASPOON SOY SAUCE	5
½ TEASPOON SESAME SEEDS	13
TOTAL	66

Preparing my meal

Steam the broccoli florets for 7 minutes, then drop them into iced water to stop the cooking. Drain and let dry on paper towels. Meanwhile, make a dressing by mixing the rice vinegar, soy sauce, and pepper. Serve the broccoli sprinkled with the sesame seeds and the dressing.

It's ready!

Variation: Sprinkle the broccoli (hot or cold) with olive oil and freshly grated Parmesan cheese.

1 TEASPOON OLIVE OIL	45
1½ TEASPOONS (⅛ OZ/5 G) PARMESAN CHEESE	22
TOTAL	133

GREEN SALAD
WITH HERBS, PURE & SIMPLE

66 *calories*

SERVES 1

PREPARATION TIME: 10 MINUTES

INGREDIENTS	CALORIES
1 LARGE HANDFUL (1 OZ/25 G) MIXED SALAD LEAVES	7
2 CILANTRO SPRIGS	2
2 CHERVIL SPRIGS	1
1 TARRAGON SPRIG	1
1 BASIL SPRIG	1
1 MINT SPRIG	1
1 TEASPOON SOY SAUCE	5
1 TEASPOON LIME JUICE	2
1 TEASPOON OLIVE OIL	45
½ TEASPOON GRATED ZEST FROM AN ORGANIC LIME	1
TOTAL	**66**

Preparing my meal

Dry the salad leaves. Pluck the leaves off all the fresh herbs. Make a dressing by mixing the soy sauce, lime juice, olive oil, 1 teaspoon water, and pepper. Combine the salad leaves and herbs and add the dressing. Toss and sprinkle with lime zest before eating.

It's ready!

This is the salad that goes with everything:

3¹/₂ oz (100 g) beef tenderloin (150 calories), seared for 1 minute on each side, thinly sliced, then sprinkled with 1¹/₂ teaspoons (¹/₈ oz/5 g) freshly grated Parmesan cheese (22 calories) and covered with salad.
TOTAL 238

3¹/₂ oz (100 g) cod fillet (80 calories), or another firm white fish, steamed for 10–12 minutes.
TOTAL 146

1 large soft-boiled egg (90 calories), cooked for 5–6 minutes in boiling water, peeled under cold running water, and broken on top of the salad.
TOTAL 156

3¹/₂ oz (100 g) cooked shrimp (80 calories), peeled. Combine with the salad and add a ¹/₂-inch (1-cm) piece of ginger, grated (2 calories).
TOTAL 148

3¹/₂ oz (100 g) chicken breast (120 calories), browned for 2 minutes each side in a frying pan over medium-high heat, then cooked for a further 5 minutes, covered, over low heat.
TOTAL 186

LEEKS
& LICORICE ROOT

202 *calories*

SERVES 1
PREPARATION TIME: 10 MINUTES
COOKING TIME: 10 MINUTES

INGREDIENTS	CALORIES
5½ OZ (150 G) LEEK	84
1 MEDIUM EGG, ABOUT 2¼ OZ (60 G)	71
1 TEASPOON OLIVE OIL	45
FLEUR DE SEL (FINE SEA SALT)	
1 STICK LICORICE ROOT	2
TOTAL	**202**

GLUTEN-FREE ◆

Preparing my meal

Prepare the leek: Cut off the root end and the top of the green section (about two-thirds), slice completely through lengthwise, and wash thoroughly. Steam for 10 minutes. Meanwhile, soft-boil the egg for 5–6 minutes in boiling water, then peel it under cold running water. Serve the leeks lukewarm, drizzled with a little olive oil and sprinkled with sea salt and pepper. Grate the licorice root over the top and add the soft-boiled egg.

It's ready!

Variations: Replace the leeks with alternative vegetables.

7 OZ (200 G) GREEN BEANS, STEAMED FOR 10–15 MINUTES	62
TOTAL	**180**
7 OZ (200 G) BROCCOLI, STEAMED FOR 7 MINUTES	64
TOTAL	**182**
5½ OZ (150 G) PEAS, STEAMED FOR 10–15 MINUTES	120
TOTAL	**238**

Extra light version: Leave out the egg.

TOTAL 131

Shopping: You can find a stick of licorice root at a health-food store or online and use a Microplane grater to make a licorice powder. A little goes a long way, and it's delicious!

Tip: If you don't like licorice, replace it with a pinch of vanilla powder, cumin, Espelette pepper, chili powder, curry powder…the choice is yours!

GRILLED
GREEN BEANS

126 *calories*

SERVES 1
PREPARATION TIME: 10 MINUTES
COOKING TIME: 20 MINUTES

INGREDIENTS	CALORIES
5½ OZ (150 G) GREEN BEANS	47
1 TEASPOON OLIVE OIL	45
8 CHERRY TOMATOES, ABOUT 3½ OZ (100 G), CHOPPED	18
½ ONION, ABOUT 1¾ OZ (50 G), THINLY SLICED	14
3 FLAT-LEAF PARSLEY SPRIGS, CHOPPED	2
TOTAL	**126**

GLUTEN-FREE ◆

Preparing my meal
Cook the green beans in a large quantity of boiling salted water for 10 minutes. Drain and pat dry. Heat the olive oil in a large frying pan, add the beans, tomatoes, and onion, and cook over medium heat for 10 minutes, stirring occasionally. Season with salt and pepper and scatter the parsley over at serving time.

It's ready!

Note from Delphine: It's not necessarily good for you, but if you let the vegetables burn a little, it produces a slightly charred flavor that is really delicious. In the end, it's a question of taste!

Extra: For a more complete meal, serve with chicken breast, steamed for 10 minutes.

1 BONELESS, SKINLESS CHICKEN BREAST, ABOUT 4¼ OZ (120 G)	144
TOTAL	**270**

TUNA DIP
& CRUDITÉS

206 *calories*

SERVES 1

PREPARATION TIME: 15 MINUTES

INGREDIENTS	CALORIES
2½ OZ (75 G) CANNED TUNA IN WATER, DRAINED	87
3 TABLESPOONS LOW-FAT PLAIN YOGURT	21
2 TEASPOONS CAPERS, ABOUT ¼ OZ (8 G)	2
6 CHIVES, SNIPPED	2
2 BASIL SPRIGS, CHOPPED	2
6 BELGIAN ENDIVE LEAVES, ABOUT 1¾ OZ (50 G)	9
½ CUCUMBER, ABOUT 7 OZ (200 G)	24
1 CARROT, ABOUT 3½ OZ (100 G)	41
8 CHERRY TOMATOES, ABOUT 3½ OZ (100 G)	18
DIP TOTAL	114
VEGETABLE TOTAL	92
TOTAL	206

GLUTEN-FREE ◆

Preparing my meal

Make the dip: Flake the tuna with a fork and add the yogurt, capers, chives, basil, and salt and pepper. Set aside in the refrigerator. Prepare the vegetables: trim the endive leaves, cut the cucumber into sticks, and peel the carrot.

It's ready!

Seasonal variation: You can give variety to this dish by using different vegetables. Add 3½ oz (100 g) of the following alternatives:

- black radish (20 calories)
- fennel (31 calories)
- raw zucchini (17 calories)
- cauliflower (25 calories)

Dip variation 1: Add 1 teaspoon mustard (5 calories) and 1 pinch curry powder (1 calorie).

DIP TOTAL 120

Dip variation 2: Add the grated zest and juice of ½ lime (5 calories) and a ¼-inch (5-mm) piece of ginger, grated (1 calorie).

DIP TOTAL 120

INDIAN-STYLE
SPINACH

172 *calories*

SERVES 1
PREPARATION TIME: 15 MINUTES
COOKING TIME: 17 MINUTES

INGREDIENTS	CALORIES
10 OZ (300 G) SPINACH	70
CANOLA OIL SPRAY	2
½ ONION, ABOUT 1¾ OZ (50 G), SLICED	14
½ TEASPOON GROUND CUMIN	2
1 CARDAMOM SEED	1
½ TEASPOON GROUND CINNAMON	3
1 BAY LEAF	1
1 CLOVE	1
1 MEDIUM TOMATO, ABOUT 3½ OZ (100 G), COARSELY CHOPPED	18
½ GARLIC CLOVE, CRUSHED	2
½-INCH (1-CM) PIECE OF GINGER, GRATED	2
½ TEASPOON GROUND TURMERIC	2
1 TABLESPOON KETCHUP	10
1½ TABLESPOONS (¾ FL OZ/25 ML) SOY CREAM (FOR COOKING) OR LOW-FAT PLAIN YOGURT	43
6 CILANTRO SPRIGS, CHOPPED	3
TOTAL	174

GLUTEN-FREE ◆

Preparing my meal

Pick over the spinach, removing the stems and any damaged leaves, then chop it coarsely. Heat a wok or large frying pan over medium heat, spray with oil, and add the onion, cumin, cardamom, cinnamon, bay leaf, clove, tomato, garlic, and ginger. Cook, stirring, for 2 minutes. Add the spinach, raise the heat to high, and stir and cook for 3 minutes. Reduce the heat to medium and cook until it turns a dark green, a further 7 minutes. Sprinkle with turmeric and stir in the ketchup and soy cream. Cook over medium heat, stirring, for 5 minutes. Before serving, scatter the cilantro over. Taste and season with salt and pepper if necessary.

It's ready!

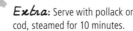

Extra: Serve with pollack or cod, steamed for 10 minutes.

4¼ OZ (120 G) POLLACK	108
TOTAL	282

ARTICHOKE
WITH THAI VINAIGRETTE

133 *calories*

SERVES 1
PREPARATION TIME: 10 MINUTES
COOKING TIME: 30 MINUTES

INGREDIENTS	CALORIES
1 GLOBE ARTICHOKE	76
1 TEASPOON OLIVE OIL	45
1 TEASPOON SOY SAUCE	5
½ TEASPOON GRATED GINGER	2
2 TEASPOONS COCONUT WATER	2
⅓ SMALL SHALLOT, CHOPPED	2
1 CILANTRO SPRIG, CHOPPED	1
TOTAL	133

Preparing my meal
Cook the artichoke in simmering salted water for about 30 minutes; it is ready when one of the outer leaves can be detached easily. Drain and allow to cool until lukewarm. Make a quick Thai vinaigrette by putting the olive oil, soy sauce, ginger, coconut water, shallot, cilantro, and pepper into a jam jar. Shake and it's ready! Pull off the artichoke leaves as you eat, starting from the outside, and dunk them into the sauce. Then, extricate the heart of the artichoke, remove the fuzzy "choke," and pour the rest of the dressing over.

It's ready!

Tip: You can also cook the artichoke in a pressure cooker. In that case, allow 10 minutes simmering time or 12 minutes steaming time from when the pressure valve starts to rotate.

Extra: Serve with a shrimp and baby spinach salad dressed with 1 teaspoon olive oil, salt, and pepper.

3½ OZ (100 G) COOKED SHRIMP	80
1 HANDFUL (1 OZ/25 G) BABY SPINACH	6
1 TEASPOON OLIVE OIL	45
TOTAL	264

Vinaigrette variation: For a more traditional vinaigrette, mix together olive oil, white wine vinegar, mustard, and salt and pepper. Thin out with a teaspoon of water if necessary.

1 TEASPOON OLIVE OIL	45
½ TEASPOON VINEGAR	1
½ TEASPOON MUSTARD	3
TOTAL	125

Green version: Replace the artichoke with broccoli, steamed for 7 minutes, and serve with the Thai vinaigrette and sesame seeds.

4¼ OZ (120 G) BROCCOLI	41
½ TEASPOON SESAME SEEDS	13
THAI VINAIGRETTE	57
TOTAL	111

MISO SOUP
REVISITED

33 *calories*

SERVES 1

PREPARATION TIME: 15 MINUTES

COOKING TIME: 10 MINUTES

INGREDIENTS	CALORIES
1 SCANT TEASPOON MISO PASTE	6
1 TEASPOON SOY SAUCE	5
½-INCH (1-CM) PIECE OF GINGER, GRATED	2
1 TEASPOON LIME JUICE	2
½ GREEN ONION, SLICED	2
½ OZ (15 G) WATERCRESS, WASHED	2
½ OZ (15 G) ASPARAGUS, PEELED AND CUT INTO SMALL PIECES	4
½ OZ (15 G) FRESH SHIITAKE MUSHROOMS, STEMMED AND BRUSHED	4
3 DROPS SESAME OIL	6
TOTAL	33

Preparing my soup

Combine the miso paste with 3 tablespoons boiling water in a saucepan. Gradually add 1 cup (8 fl oz/250 ml) boiling water, stirring. Add the soy sauce, ginger, lime juice, and a tiny pinch of salt and some pepper, and bring to a boil. Simmer very gently for 5 minutes. Add the green onion, watercress, asparagus, and mushrooms. Pour into a bowl and sprinkle with sesame oil. Season with salt and pepper again, if necessary.

It's ready!

Extra: Add silken tofu just before the soup is done, simmering gently to warm it.

3½ OZ (100 G) TOFU 120

TOTAL 153

Tip: If you can't find fresh shiitake mushrooms, you can use dried ones instead. Weigh them *after* rehydrating them!

GREEN SOUP
& TOFU

113 *calories*

SERVES 1

PREPARATION TIME: 10 MINUTES

COOKING TIME: 22 MINUTES

INGREDIENTS	CALORIES
1¾ OZ (50 G) SWISS CHARD LEAVES, COARSELY CHOPPED	7
1¾ OZ (50 G) KALE LEAVES, COARSELY CHOPPED	25
½-INCH (1-CM) PIECE OF GINGER, GRATED	2
½ GARLIC CLOVE, CHOPPED	2
1¾ OZ (50 G) TOFU, DICED	60
1 CILANTRO SPRIG, CHOPPED	1
1 FLAT-LEAF PARSLEY SPRIG, CHOPPED	1
½ TEASPOON SESAME SEEDS	13
¼ LIME	2
TOTAL	**113**

GLUTEN-FREE ◆

Preparing my soup

Wilt the chard and kale leaves in a medium saucepan for 2 minutes, stirring. Add the ginger, garlic, 1 cup (8 fl oz/250 ml) boiling water, and salt and pepper. Cook for 10 minutes, then let cool slightly before blending. Return the soup to the saucepan, add the tofu, and cook for a further 10 minutes over low heat. Pour into a bowl, add the chopped cilantro and parsley, and sprinkle with the sesame seeds. Serve with the lime quarter to squeeze over the top.

It's ready!

Variation: Replace the Swiss chard with mâche (also known as corn salad or lamb's lettuce) (18 calories) and the kale with napa cabbage (6 calories).

TOTAL 105

GAZPACHO

139 *calories*

SERVES 1
PREPARATION TIME: 15 MINUTES
REFRIGERATION TIME: 2 HOURS

INGREDIENTS	CALORIES
2 TOMATOES, ABOUT 5½ OZ (150 G)	27
⅓ CUCUMBER, ABOUT 4½ OZ (125 G)	15
¼ GREEN BELL PEPPER, ABOUT 1¾ OZ (50 G)	17
¼ RED BELL PEPPER, ABOUT 1¾ OZ (50 G), SEEDED	17
½ ONION, SLICED	14
½ GARLIC CLOVE, CHOPPED	2
1 TABLESPOON WINE VINEGAR	2
1 TEASPOON OLIVE OIL	45
TOTAL	139

GLUTEN-FREE ◆

Preparing my soup

Chop the tomatoes, cucumber, and bell peppers. Purée with the onion, garlic, vinegar, and olive oil to a smooth soup consistency. Season with salt and pepper. Refrigerate for at least 2 hours so it's well chilled. Serve with ice cubes.

It's ready!

Tip: You can pass the soup through a chinois or fine sieve before putting it in the refrigerator.

Variation: Another version of gazpacho that's different and so good. The method is the same. It is best to pass the soup through a chinois or fine sieve before serving.

⅓ CUCUMBER	15
¼ AVOCADO	80
½ GRANNY SMITH APPLE	40
1 GREEN ONION	3
JUICE OF ½ LIME	4
2 CILANTRO SPRIGS	2
1 BASIL SPRIG	1
1 FLAT-LEAF PARSLEY SPRIG	1
½-INCH (1-CM) PIECE GINGER, GRATED	2
1 TEASPOON OLIVE OIL	45
TOTAL	193

TOMATO
& GOAT CHEESE SALAD

163 calories

SERVES 1

PREPARATION TIME: 10 MINUTES

INGREDIENTS	CALORIES
9 OZ (250 G) FIRM SEASONAL TOMATOES, CUT INTO WEDGES	45
1 OZ (25 G) ASHED GOAT CHEESE	65
1 TEASPOON OLIVE OIL	45
1 TEASPOON BALSAMIC VINEGAR	5
2 CHIVES, SNIPPED	1
1 BASIL SPRIG, LEAVES PICKED	1
1 MINT SPRIG, LEAVES PICKED	1
TOTAL	**163**

GLUTEN-FREE ◆

Preparing my meal

Arrange the tomato wedges on a plate with the piece of goat cheese. Drizzle with olive oil and vinegar, sprinkle with salt, and give a turn of the pepper mill. Add the herbs and serve immediately.

It's ready!

Delphine's advice: This salad is excellent with whatever tomatoes are at their peak of season; choose them in a few different colors!

AL DENTE
QUINOA

150 calories

MAKES ½ CUP (3 OZ/85 G); SERVES 1

COOKING TIME: 7 MINUTES

RESTING TIME: 5 MINUTES

INGREDIENTS	CALORIES
¼ CUP (1½ OZ/40 G) QUINOA	150
TOTAL	150

Rinse the quinoa and cook it in one and a half times its volume of boiling salted water for 7 minutes. Let the quinoa stand off the heat for 5 minutes. It should be perfectly cooked—light, crunchy, fluffy, and delicious.

Variation: For a spiced version, add 1 pinch cumin (1 calorie), 1 pinch saffron (1 calorie) and ¼ preserved lemon (5 calories), rinsed, seeded, and chopped into small cubes, to the cooking water; don't add salt.

Tip: Quinoa will double in volume after cooking. Cook two to three servings to keep on hand in the refrigerator, where it will keep for 3–6 days.

HOME-COOKED
KIDNEY BEANS

MAKES EIGHT ¾-CUP (3¾-OZ/110-G) SERVINGS

COOKING TIME: 1 HOUR 30 MINUTES MAXIMUM

SOAKING TIME: OVERNIGHT

INGREDIENTS	CALORIES
2 CUPS (12½ OZ/360 G) DRIED KIDNEY BEANS WILL MAKE 8 SERVINGS COOKED BEANS	
PER SERVING	142

Soak the beans in cold water overnight in the refrigerator. Rinse, drain, and combine in a saucepan with three times their volume of cold water. Heat to a simmer, then reduce the heat to a very low simmer and allow 1–1½ hours cooking time, depending on how firm you want them to be. Add more water if beans start to look dry. Season once they're cooked.

Variation: For a more flavored version, add 1 clove (1 calorie), ¼ onion, chopped (7 calories), 1 thyme sprig (1 calorie), and 1 small bay leaf (1 calorie) to the cooking water.

Tip: Dried beans will triple their volume when cooked. Prepare extra servings to keep in the refrigerator for up to 3 days, or in the freezer for several months.

PERFECT
WHOLE BLACK RICE

MAKES ½ CUP (3¼ OZ/90 G); SERVES 1

COOKING TIME: 1 HOUR MAXIMUM

INGREDIENTS	CALORIES
¼ CUP (1½ OZ/45 G) WHOLE BLACK RICE	150
TOTAL	150

Fill a large pot with water and add the rice. Bring to a boil, add salt, stir, and cook over medium-high heat, uncovered, for about 40 minutes. The rice should open and show its pale interior, but the grains should not curve—this is a sign of overcooking. Drain, return the rice to the pan, cover, and let steam for 10 minutes before serving.

Variation: For a spicy version, add 1 small red chile (1 calorie) to the cooking water.

Tip: If you don't like whole black rice, replace it with ¼ cup (1½ oz/45 g) brown basmati rice (150 calories), cooked according to the packet instructions. White rice has a higher glycemic index, so it should be consumed in moderation. Do try whole black rice though—it's so good. You will find it easily in organic food stores or online.

Warning: Don't keep cooked rice in the refrigerator for more than a day or two, as it could develop harmful bacteria.

MUSSEL
SALAD

262 calories

SERVES 1

PREPARATION TIME: 20 MINUTES

COOKING TIME: 10 MINUTES

INGREDIENTS	CALORIES
10 OZ (300 G) MUSSELS IN THEIR SHELLS, SCRUBBED AND DEBEARDED	128
1 SMALL SHALLOT, CHOPPED	7
1 TABLESPOON WHITE WINE	8
1 TEASPOON OLIVE OIL	45
1 TEASPOON CIDER VINEGAR	2
⅓ CUP (1¾ OZ/50 G) COOKED OR CANNED KIDNEY BEANS (SEE NOTE)	64
1 GREEN ONION, THINLY SLICED	3
3 FLAT-LEAF PARSLEY SPRIGS, CHOPPED	2
TOTAL	259

GLUTEN-FREE ♦

Preparing my meal

Heat a large frying pan and add the mussels with the shallot, ¼ cup (2 fl oz/50 ml) water, the white wine, olive oil, salt and pepper. Cover and cook, shaking the frying pan from time to time, until all the shells are open, about 5 minutes. (Discard any mussels whose shells do not open.) Drain the mussels, collecting the cooking juices. Strain the juice, add the cider vinegar, and place over medium heat for 5 minutes to reduce by half. Rinse the kidney beans, then put them into a large bowl. Add the mussels, green onion, and parsley, and dress with the juices. Mix together, taste, and adjust the salt and pepper if necessary.

It's ready!

Home-cooked beans: Follow the instructions on page 124 to cook dried beans before using.

"Super 500" version: Double the quantities, with the exception of the olive oil, to make a super easy "Super 500" dish.

TOTAL 479

"Super 500" variation for men: Triple the quantity of kidney beans, and double the rest.

SCANT 1 CUP (5½ OZ/150 G) 190
COOKED OR CANNED BEANS

TOTAL 575

FLASH-SEARED TUNA

180 calories

SERVES 1
PREPARATION TIME: 10 MINUTES
MARINATING TIME: 1 HOUR
COOKING TIME: 2 MINUTES

INGREDIENTS	CALORIES
3½ OZ (100 G) VERY FRESH RAW BLUEFIN TUNA	108
1 TEASPOON OLIVE OIL	45
1 TEASPOON SOY SAUCE	5
1 TEASPOON RICE VINEGAR	2
⅓ TEASPOON AGAVE SYRUP	8
1 HANDFUL (1 OZ/25 G) BABY SPINACH	6
¾ OZ (20 G) SPROUTS (SUCH AS CABBAGE OR ALFALFA)	6
TOTAL	180

Preparing my meal

Marinate the tuna in a mixture of the olive oil, soy sauce, rice vinegar, agave syrup, and pepper. Refrigerate for 1 hour, turning the tuna over from time to time. Combine the spinach with the sprouts. Heat a frying pan over high heat and sear the tuna for 1 minute on each side: it needs to stay very red inside. Place the tuna on a plate, cover with spinach and sprouts, and pour the rest of the marinade over. Season with salt and pepper, if necessary.

It's ready!

 Tip: For something a little different, you can replace the baby spinach with purslane or arugula—the calories are the same.

 Raw version: Slice the tuna very thinly, sprinkle with the marinade, refrigerate for 1 hour, then serve with the mixed salad on top.

CEVICHE

191 calories

SERVES 1

PREPARATION TIME: 15 MINUTES

MARINATING TIME: 2 HOURS

INGREDIENTS	CALORIES
¼ RED CHILE	1
GRATED ZEST AND JUICE OF ½ ORGANIC LIME	5
3 CILANTRO SPRIGS, CHOPPED	2
1 FLAT-LEAF PARSLEY SPRIG, CHOPPED	1
1 GREEN ONION, THINLY SLICED	3
3½ OZ (100 G) VERY FRESH RAW SEA BASS FILLET, OR OTHER FIRM WHITE FISH	125
4 CHERRY TOMATOES, ABOUT 1¾ OZ (50 G)	9
1 TEASPOON OLIVE OIL	45
TOTAL	191

GLUTEN-FREE ◆

Preparing my meal

Finely chop the chile and remove the seeds (don't put too much chile in—it's better to add more later if needed!). Make a marinade with the lime zest and juice, half the chopped herbs, the green onion, and the chile. Clean and dry the fish and cut it into small pieces. Put the pieces in a dish and pour the marinade over. Refrigerate for at least 2 hours (the longer the fish stays in the refrigerator, the more it will "cook"). Cut the tomatoes in half, remove the soft pulp, and chop the flesh into small pieces. Add the tomato pieces to the ceviche, season very lightly with salt and pepper, and scatter the rest of the chopped herbs over with a little olive oil. Serve immediately.

It's ready!

Variation: Replace the sea bass with very fresh raw sea bream, cod, or salmon.

3½ OZ (100 G) SEA BREAM	100
TOTAL	166
3½ OZ (100 G) COD	80
TOTAL	146
3½ OZ (100 G) SALMON	166
TOTAL	232

STEAMED FISH

& CRISP GREEN BEANS

SERVES 1

PREPARATION TIME: 20 MINUTES

COOKING TIME: 20 MINUTES

INGREDIENTS	CALORIES
3½ OZ (100 G) GREEN BEANS, TRIMMED	31
1 SMALL SHALLOT, FINELY CHOPPED	7
4¼ OZ (120 G) COD FILLET, OR OTHER FIRM WHITE FISH	96
4 CHERRY TOMATOES, ABOUT 1¾ OZ (50 G)	9
1 TEASPOON LEMON JUICE	2
2 BLACK OLIVES, PITTED	13
4 BASIL LEAVES	1
TOTAL	**159**

GLUTEN-FREE ◆

Preparing my meal

Put the green beans and shallot in a steamer basket and steam for 20 minutes. After 10 minutes, add the fish fillet. Purée the tomatoes with the lemon juice, olives, basil, some salt and pepper, and 2 tablespoons water. Check to see if the fish is cooked (it should take on a pearly color and flake if prodded with a fork). Serve the fish and beans dressed with the tomato sauce.

It's ready!

Variation: Replace the cod with fillets of red mullet and place them on the green beans 5 minutes before the end of the cooking time.

4¼ OZ (120 G) RED MULLET (OR TRY SEA BASS OR OCEAN PERCH)	111
TOTAL	**174**

Extra: Serve this dish with brown basmati rice (see page 90 for instructions).

2½ TABLESPOONS (1 OZ/30 G) UNCOOKED BASMATI RICE	105
COD VERSION TOTAL	**264**
RED MULLET VERSION TOTAL	**279**

159 calories

SCALLOPS
& MUSHROOMS

156 *calories*

SERVES 1

PREPARATION TIME: 15 MINUTES

COOKING TIME: 15 MINUTES

INGREDIENTS	CALORIES
4–6 SCALLOPS ON THE SHELL, ABOUT 4¼ OZ (120 G)	104
1¾ OZ (50 G) CHANTERELLE MUSHROOMS	10
1 SMALL SHALLOT, CHOPPED	7
1 TARRAGON SPRIG, LEAVES PICKED	1
1 TEASPOON (⅛ OZ/5 G) LIGHTLY SALTED BUTTER	34
FLEUR DE SEL (FINE SEA SALT)	
TOTAL	156

GLUTEN-FREE ◆

Preparing my meal

Ask the fishmonger to prepare the scallops: cleaned, coral removed, on their shells but detached. Arrange 2 scallops on each shell. Trim the mushroom stems and clean the mushrooms gently with a damp cloth. Cut the largest ones into a few pieces. Preheat the oven to 350°F (180°C). Divide the shallot and tarragon leaves among the shells. Add the mushrooms directly to the shells. Dot with small pieces of butter, sprinkle with sea salt, and give a turn of the pepper mill. Roast for 15 minutes.

It's ready!

Extra: Serve with a bowl of whole black rice (see page 124 for cooking instructions).

¼ CUP (1½ OZ/45 G) UNCOOKED BLACK RICE	150
TOTAL	306

Note from Delphine: I love this recipe, with its mixture of briny and earthy flavors!

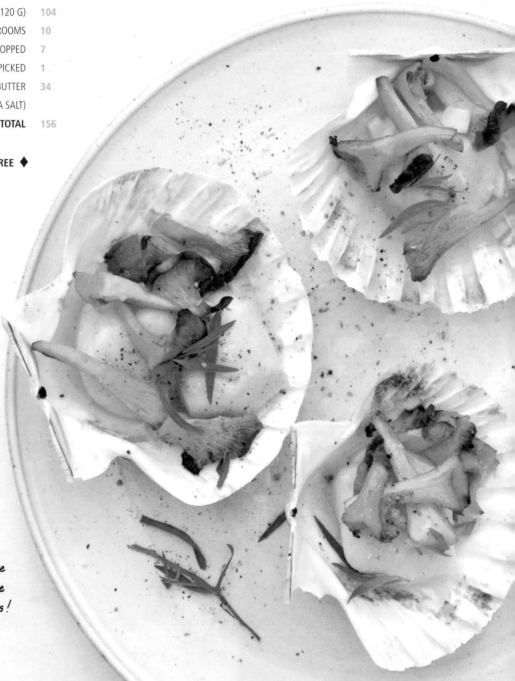

FISH TARTARE
& MANGO

179 calories

SERVES 1

PREPARATION TIME: 15 MINUTES

INGREDIENTS	CALORIES
3½ OZ (100 G) VERY FRESH RAW SEA BREAM	100
¼ MANGO, ABOUT 1 OZ (30 G)	20
½-INCH (1-CM) PIECE OF GINGER, GRATED	2
5 CILANTRO SPRIGS, LEAVES CHOPPED	3
3 MINT LEAVES, CHOPPED	1
1 HANDFUL (1 OZ/25 G) BEAN SPROUTS	8
1 TEASPOON OLIVE OIL	45
FLEUR DE SEL (FINE SEA SALT)	
TOTAL	179

GLUTEN-FREE ◆

Preparing my meal

Dice the fish and mango and combine them in a bowl. Add the ginger, cilantro, mint, and the bean sprouts, cut into short lengths. Dress with the olive oil, season lightly with sea salt, and add some pepper. Mix together and refrigerate before serving.

It's ready!

Variation: Replace the bream with very fresh salmon. It's also very good but has significantly more calories.

3½ OZ (100 G) RAW SALMON	166
TOTAL	245

Tip: Wait a little while before eating the tartare—it tastes better.

Less sweet version:
Replace the mango with thinly sliced pink radishes.

1 OZ (30 G) PINK RADISH	6
TOTAL	165

ZUCCHINI
& SHRIMP

148 calories

SERVES 1

PREPARATION TIME: 10 MINUTES

MARINATING TIME: 30 MINUTES (OPTIONAL)

INGREDIENTS	CALORIES
½ ZUCCHINI, ABOUT 4½ OZ (125 G), THINLY SLICED	21
3½ OZ (100 G) COOKED SHRIMP, PEELED	80
1 TARRAGON SPRIG, LEAVES PICKED	1
1 TEASPOON OLIVE OIL	45
GRATED ZEST OF ½ ORGANIC LIME	1
TOTAL	148

GLUTEN-FREE ◆

Preparing my meal

Put the zucchini slices and shrimp in a bowl. Add the tarragon leaves, olive oil, and salt and pepper. Mix and let marinate in the refrigerator for 30 minutes before serving, for best flavor. Sprinkle with the lime zest just before serving.

It's ready!

Variation: Add some freshly grated Parmesan cheese along with the zest.

1 TABLESPOON (¼ OZ/10 G) PARMESAN CHEESE	44
TOTAL	192

Extra nutritious variation: Add some arugula, quinoa, and chickpeas. (See page 124 for how to cook quinoa.)

1 HANDFUL (1 OZ/25 G) ARUGULA	6
2½ TABLESPOONS (1 OZ/25 G) UNCOOKED QUINOA	147
3 TABLESPOONS (1 OZ/30 G) CANNED CHICKPEAS	111
TOTAL	412

FISH
WITH A THAI JUS

213 *calories*

SERVES 1
PREPARATION TIME: 10 MINUTES
COOKING TIME: 35 MINUTES

INGREDIENTS	CAL
1 SMALL SHALLOT, CHOPPED	7
½-INCH (1-CM) PIECE OF GINGER, GRATED	2
4 KAFFIR LIME LEAVES OR 1 LEMONGRASS STALK	2
½ GARLIC CLOVE	2
5 CILANTRO SPRIGS, CHOPPED	3
1 SMALL RED CHILE	2
JUICE OF ½ LIME	4
1 OZ (25 G) RICE VERMICELLI	91
3½ OZ (100 G) COD FILLET, OR OTHER FIRM WHITE FISH	100
TOTAL	213

GLUTEN-FREE ◆

Preparing my meal

Make a stock with 3 cups (24 fl oz/750 ml) water, the shallot, ginger, kaffir lime leaves or lemongrass (trimmed and cut into short lengths), the garlic, cilantro, chile, lime juice, and salt. Cook on a gentle simmer for 30 minutes. Add the rice vermicelli and fish, and cook for 5 minutes over low heat. Place the vermicelli and fish in a deep plate, add a few tablespoons of broth, and season lightly with salt and pepper.

It's ready!

Extra: For a more complete meal, add green beans, steamed for 10–15 minutes.

3½ OZ (100 G) GREEN BEANS	31
TOTAL	244

GRILLED SQUID
WITH LEMON

SERVES 1
PREPARATION TIME: 15 MINUTES
MARINATING TIME: 1 HOUR (OPTIONAL)
COOKING TIME: 2 MINUTES

157
calories

INGREDIENTS	CALORIES
3½ OZ (100 G) CLEANED SQUID	92
GRATED ZEST AND JUICE OF 1 ORGANIC LIME	10
1 TEASPOON OLIVE OIL	45
½ GARLIC CLOVE	2
FLEUR DE SEL (FINE SEA SALT)	
1 LARGE HANDFUL (1 OZ/25 G) ARUGULA	6
2 BASIL SPRIGS, LEAVES PICKED	2
TOTAL	157

GLUTEN-FREE ◆

Preparing my meal

Slice the squid tubes into strips, chop the tentacles into small pieces, and rinse and dry well. Marinate the squid pieces in a mixture of the lime juice, olive oil, garlic, and a little sea salt and pepper. Let marinate in the refrigerator for 1 hour, if desired. Pat the arugula and basil dry and combine. Drain the squid, reserving the marinade. Heat a frying pan over high heat until very hot and sear the squid for 1 minute to brown well. Continue cooking for 1 minute, stirring constantly. Serve sprinkled with lime zest and accompanied with the salad dressed with the rest of the marinade.

It's ready!

Tip: Be careful when cooking the squid: the longer you cook it, the more rubbery it becomes. Make sure the frying pan is very hot so it sears rather than stews.

Extra: Cook some pasta (such as spaghetti or penne) until al dente, refresh it under cold water, drain, and toss with the salad while still warm. Yum, yum.

2¼ OZ (60 G) PASTA	207
TOTAL	364

BLINI
& SMOKED SALMON

284 *calories*

SERVES 1

PREPARATION TIME: 20 MINUTES

COOKING TIME: 1 MINUTE

INGREDIENTS	CALORIES
2 TABLESPOONS (¾ OZ/20 G) OAT BRAN	49
1 TABLESPOON (¼ OZ/10 G) LOW-FAT FROMAGE BLANC (ALTERNATIVELY, USE QUARK OR YOGURT CHEESE)	8
1 SMALL EGG	54
6 CHIVES, SNIPPED	2
2 DROPS OLIVE OIL	5
1 TABLESPOON (½ FL OZ/20 ML) SOY CREAM OR LIGHT SOUR CREAM, WELL CHILLED	34
2½ OZ (70 G) SMOKED SALMON	126
GRATED ZEST OF ½ ORGANIC LEMON	6
TOTAL	284

Preparing my meal

Combine the oat bran with the fromage blanc, add the egg, and whisk together. Then add half the chives and a little salt and pepper. Grease a frying pan with the olive oil, wiping it over the base with a paper towel—it's just so the blini doesn't stick and browns a little. Heat the frying pan and pour in the batter, spreading it out to a pancake shape. Cook for 30 seconds on each side. Whisk the soy cream to make it more light and frothy. Lightly season with salt. Serve the blini with topped with the smoked salmon and cream and sprinkled with lemon zest, the rest of the chives, and pepper.

It's ready!

Variation: Replace the smoked salmon with salmon roe.

1¾ OZ (50 G) SALMON ROE	126
TOTAL	284

Shopping: If you can't find soy cream, you can use light crème fraîche instead—it has the same number of calories. Or, light sour cream: it has even fewer.

SEAFOOD
& BROTH

238 *calories*

SERVES 1

PREPARATION TIME: 20 MINUTES

COOKING TIME: 20 MINUTES

INGREDIENTS	CALORIES
2–3 SCALLOPS, ABOUT 2½ OZ (60 G)	52
1¾ OZ (50 G) SMOKED MACKEREL, HERRING, TROUT, OR OTHER FATTY, FLAKY-TEXTURED FISH	82
1 OZ (25 G) JERUSALEM ARTICHOKE	18
1 OZ (25 G) KOHLRABI	10
½ TEASPOON BLACK SESAME SEEDS	13
1 TEASPOON PUMPKIN SEED OIL	45
4 KAFFIR LIME LEAVES OR 1 LEMONGRASS STALK	2
1 SMALL SHALLOT, CHOPPED	7
½-INCH (1-CM) PIECE OF GINGER, GRATED	2
½ GARLIC CLOVE	2
6 CILANTRO SPRIGS, LEAVES AND STEMS, CHOPPED	3
1 SMALL RED CHILE	2
TOTAL	238

GLUTEN-FREE ♦

Preparing my meal

Clean the scallops and mackerel and chop them into small cubes (as for a ceviche). Peel the Jerusalem artichoke and kohlrabi, and chop them into small cubes. Combine with the scallops and fish. Salt lightly, season with pepper, add the sesame seeds and pumpkin seed oil, combine, and set aside in the refrigerator. If using lemongrass, remove the outer layer and trim the base, then cut the more tender part into short lengths, stopping as soon as it becomes woody. In a medium saucepan, make a broth with 2 cups (16 fl oz/500 ml) water, the shallot, ginger, kaffir lime leaves or lemongrass, the garlic, half the cilantro, the chile, and some salt. Cook on a gentle simmer for 20 minutes, then strain. Taste and adjust the salt and pepper if necessary. At serving time, pour the very hot broth over the fish and vegetable mixture, and scatter the rest of the cilantro over.

It's ready!

Delphine's advice: If you can't find Jerusalem artichokes and kohlrabi, replace them with diced raw zucchini.

100 G (3½ OZ) ZUCCHINI	17
TOTAL	227

Variation: Replace the smoked mackerel with a white fish such as smoked cod.

1¾ OZ (50 G) SMOKED COD	40
TOTAL	196

Shopping: You can find pumpkin seed oil in organic food stores or online. Alternatively, you can replace it with olive oil or hazelnut oil.

Extra: Serve with bulgur, cooked according to the instructions on page 70.

2½ TABLESPOONS (¾ OZ/ 20 G) UNCOOKED BULGUR	206
TOTAL	444

OMELETTE
WITH HAM, TOMATO & SALAD

182
calories

SERVES 1

PREPARATION TIME: 20 MINUTES

COOKING TIME: 5 MINUTES

INGREDIENTS	CALORIES
2 SMALL EGGS	108
½ TEASPOON OLIVE OIL	23
1 PINCH GROUND CUMIN	1
4 CHERRY TOMATOES, ABOUT 1¾ OZ (50 G), CUT INTO SMALL PIECES	9
1 SLICE (1 OZ/25 G) HAM, TRIMMED OF FAT AND CHOPPED	30
1 HANDFUL (1/OZ/25 G) MIXED SALAD LEAVES	6
1 CHERVIL SPRIG, LEAVES PICKED	1
1–2 MUSHROOMS, ABOUT ½ OZ (15 G)	4
TOTAL	182

Preparing my meal

Beat the eggs with the olive oil, cumin, and salt and pepper. Place a nonstick frying pan over high heat and pour in the eggs. Let the omelette set slightly for 1 minute, reduce the heat, and top with the tomatoes and ham, then let set for another 1–2 minutes. Fold the omelette over and transfer to a plate. Mix the salad leaves and chervil, then thinly slice the mushrooms (with a mandoline if you have one) at the last moment. Serve the omelette with the salad and mushrooms on top. Season with salt and pepper.

It's ready!

Tip: Beat the eggs for quite a while so that they become nice and foamy and the omelette is very light.

Delphine's advice: Porcini mushrooms are a tasty alternative. If you're able to get fresh ones, make sure to remove any green foam from under the mushroom cap before slicing.

Indulgent variation: Dollop some ricotta on the tomato and ham.

2 TABLESPOONS (1 OZ/25 G) RICOTTA CHEESE	35
TOTAL	217

CHICKEN
BROCHETTES WITH LEMONGRASS

SERVES 1
PREPARATION TIME: 15 MINUTES
MARINATING TIME: 1 HOUR
COOKING TIME: 8 MINUTES

INGREDIENTS	CALORIES
1 LEMONGRASS STALK	2
JUICE OF 1 LIME	8
1 TEASPOON OLIVE OIL	45
1 GARLIC CLOVE, CRUSHED	4
4 CILANTRO SPRIGS, CHOPPED	2
4 MINT LEAVES, CHOPPED	2
5½ OZ (150 G) BONELESS, SKINLESS CHICKEN BREAST	180
1 TEASPOON ESPELETTE PEPPER (PIMENT D'ESPELETTE), CHILI POWDER, OR RED PEPPER FLAKES	6
TOTAL	249

GLUTEN-FREE ◆

Preparing my meal
Remove the outer layer of the lemongrass stalk and trim the base. Chop the more tender part, stopping as soon as it becomes woody. Purée the lemongrass, lime juice, olive oil, garlic, cilantro, and mint with ¼ cup (2 fl oz/60 ml) water and some pepper. Slice the chicken into roughly equal 1-inch (2.5-cm) cubes. Thread them onto skewers. Marinate the chicken in the lemongrass mixture in the refrigerator for 1 hour. Heat a frying pan over medium heat and add the brochettes (set the marinade aside). Cook them for 2 minutes on each side, cover, and cook them for a further 2 minutes over medium-low heat. Bring the marinade to a boil for 2 minutes before serving it with the brochettes sprinkled with Espelette pepper.

It's ready!

Extra: For a heartier meal, serve with quinoa (see page 124 for cooking instructions) and arugula.

3 TABLESPOONS (1 OZ/30 G) UNCOOKED QUINOA	110
25 G (1 OZ/1 HANDFUL) ARUGULA	6
TOTAL	360

244 *calories*

BEEF
MEATBALLS

246 *calories*

SERVES 1
PREPARATION TIME: 15 MINUTES
COOKING TIME: 25 MINUTES

INGREDIENTS	CALORIES
2 MEDIUM TOMATOES, ABOUT 7 OZ (200 G)	36
⅓ TEASPOON GROUND CUMIN	2
1 SMALL RED CHILE	2
5½ OZ (150 G) GROUND BEEF, 95% LEAN	193
1 SMALL SHALLOT, CHOPPED	7
½-INCH (1-CM) PIECE OF GINGER, GRATED	2
5 CILANTRO SPRIGS, CHOPPED	2
5 MINT LEAVES, CHOPPED	2
TOTAL	246

GLUTEN-FREE ◆

Preparing my meal
Purée the tomatoes with ½ cup (4 fl oz/125 ml) water, the cumin, and salt and pepper. Combine with the chile in a medium saucepan over medium-high heat and simmer for 20 minutes. Meanwhile, combine the ground beef in a bowl with the shallot, ginger, cilantro, mint, and pepper. Shape into meatballs the size of a large walnut. Brown the meatballs in a nonstick frying pan over high heat for 2 minutes, then add them to the sauce and continue cooking for 3 minutes. Remember to remove the chile from the sauce before serving!

It's ready!

Extra: For a more balanced meal, serve with kidney beans (see page 124 for cooking instructions) and baby spinach.

⅓ CUP (2 OZ/60 G) COOKED OR CANNED KIDNEY BEANS	76
25 G (1 OZ) BABY SPINACH	6
TOTAL	328

THAI TARTARE

211 *calories*

SERVES 1

PREPARATION TIME: 15 MINUTES

INGREDIENTS	CALORIES
1 LEMONGRASS STALK	2
¼ RED CHILE, SEEDED AND FINELY CHOPPED	1
1 GREEN ONION, CHOPPED	3
½-INCH (1-CM) PIECE OF GINGER, PEELED AND CUT INTO MATCHSTICKS	2
3 CILANTRO SPRIGS, CHOPPED	2
3½ OZ (100 G) VERY FRESH BEEF TENDERLOIN, CUT INTO SMALL CUBES	150
1 TEASPOON OLIVE OIL	45
½ TEASPOON FISH SAUCE	5
GRATED ZEST OF ½ ORGANIC LIME	1
TOTAL	**211**

Preparing my meal

Remove the outer layer of the lemongrass stalk and trim the base. Chop the more tender part, stopping as soon as it becomes woody. Combine the prepared vegetables and herbs with the meat, pour the olive oil and fish sauce over, mix again, and set aside in the refrigerator before serving. Sprinkle with the lime zest just before serving.

It's ready!

Tip: If you have a good butcher, simply get a piece of very fresh sirloin—it will be just as good, and have fewer calories.

3½ OZ (100 G) RUMP STEAK	136
TOTAL	**197**

Green version: Serve with arugula.

1 HANDFUL (1 OZ/25 G) ARUGULA	6
TOTAL	**217**

Extra: Serve with brown basmati rice (see page 90 for cooking instructions).

2½ TABLESPOONS (1 OZ/30 G) BROWN BASMATI RICE	105
TOTAL	**316**

NICE & SPICY

BEEF SALAD

SERVES 1

PREPARATION TIME: 10 MINUTES

COOKING TIME: 1 MINUTE

INGREDIENTS	CALORIES
5–10 DROPS TABASCO SAUCE	1
½ GREEN ONION, CHOPPED	2
2 CILANTRO SPRIGS, CHOPPED	2
1 FLAT-LEAF PARSLEY SPRIG, FINELY CHOPPED	1
GRATED ZEST AND JUICE OF ½ LIME	5
2 TEASPOONS KETCHUP	10
½ GARLIC CLOVE, CRUSHED	2
1 TEASPOON OLIVE OIL	45
1 TEASPOON SWEET AND SOUR SAUCE	5
2 LITTLE GEM OR BABY ROMAINE LETTUCE HEARTS	15
3½ OZ (100 G) BEEF TENDERLOIN	150
½ TEASPOON SESAME SEEDS	13
TOTAL	251

Preparing my meal

Make a sauce: in a bowl, combine the Tabasco sauce, green onion, cilantro, parsley, lime zest and juice, ketchup, garlic, olive oil, and sweet and sour sauce. Mix well and set aside at room temperature. Cut the lettuce hearts into wedges. Sear the meat in a frying pan over high heat for 30 seconds on each side. Slice it thinly, arrange on a plate, and sprinkle with the sesame seeds. Add the lettuce, seasoned with salt and pepper, and serve with the spicy sauce.

It's ready!

Tip: This dish is perfect to follow a "light" aperitif between friends!

251 calories

SWEET & SAVORY
BELGIAN ENDIVE

154 *calories*

SERVES 1

PREPARATION TIME: 10 MINUTES

INGREDIENTS	CALORIES
5½ OZ (150 G) BELGIAN ENDIVE	26
½ PEAR, ABOUT 3¼ OZ (90 G)	50
1 TEASPOON LEMON JUICE	2
1 SLICE (1 OZ/25 G) HAM, TRIMMED OF FAT AND CUT INTO SMALL PIECES	30
1 TARRAGON SPRIG, LEAVES PICKED	1
1 TEASPOON WALNUT OIL	45
TOTAL	154

Preparing my meal

Discard the two or three outer leaves of the endive. Trim the base and take out the central core at the bottom to remove the bitterness. Slice into strips. Peel the pear, remove the core, chop the flesh into small pieces, and sprinkle with the lemon juice. Put the endive, pear, and ham in a bowl, scatter the tarragon leaves over, dress with the walnut oil, and season with pepper and a little salt. Gently combine and serve immediately.

It's ready!

Tip: Double the amount of ham for a meal that's still less than 200 calories.

TOTAL 184

Variation: Use a fine Microplane grater to grate some aged Comté or Gruyère cheese over the salad at the last moment.

¼ OZ (10 G) AGED 40
COMTÉ CHEESE

TOTAL 194

SEARED
VEAL
& MUSHROOMS

259
calories

SERVES 1

PREPARATION TIME: 20 MINUTES

COOKING TIME: 5 MINUTES

INGREDIENTS	CALORIES
4¼ OZ (120 G) VEAL TENDERLOIN	168
1 TEASPOON OLIVE OIL	45
1 HANDFUL (1 OZ/25 G) BABY SALAD LEAVES	6
7 OZ (200 G) SEASONAL MUSHROOMS, TRIMMED AND BRUSHED	40
TOTAL	259

GLUTEN-FREE ◆

Preparing my meal

Brush both sides of the meat with olive oil. Heat a frying pan over high heat to very hot and sear the meat on one side. When the fillet has turned "white" two-thirds of the way up, set it aside, covered with foil. Tear the salad leaves and slice the mushrooms into roughly equal pieces. Reheat the frying pan over high heat, add the mushrooms, and cook for 2 minutes without stirring. Return the meat to the pan, uncooked side down, and cook for 1 minute. Season with salt and pepper and serve the veal and mushrooms with the salad leaves.

It's ready!

Tip: You can also sear the meat in a hot frying pan without any oil and sprinkle the olive oil on the salad leaves.

Note from Delphine: I love this dish, which has the flavor of the forest. Feel free to use a combination of wild mushrooms and regular mushrooms. Their caloric value will be the same.

Chapter 3

NON-FAST DAY RECIPES

ENERGY
SOUP

SERVES 4

PREPARATION TIME: 15 MINUTES

INGREDIENTS

3½ OZ (100 G) SPINACH

1 TEASPOON WAKAME SEAWEED POWDER

1 ZUCCHINI, PEELED AND COARSELY CHOPPED

⅓ CUCUMBER, PEELED , SEEDED, AND COARSELY CHOPPED

8 BASIL LEAVES

¾-INCH (2-CM) PIECE OF GINGER, GRATED

2 TABLESPOONS SOY SAUCE

1 TABLESPOON ALMOND BUTTER

FLEUR DE SEL (FINE SEA SALT)

1 TEASPOON FLAXSEEDS

1 TEASPOON PEPITAS (PUMPKIN SEEDS)

1 TEASPOON MUSTARD SEEDS

Preparing my soup

In the bowl of a mixer or a blender, combine the spinach leaves, seaweed powder, zucchini, cucumber, basil, ginger, soy sauce, almond butter, 1 cup (8 fl oz/250 ml) water, a very small amount of fine sea salt, and a little pepper. Purée, taste, and add a little more water if necessary. Combine the flaxseeds, pepitas, and mustard seeds in a small bowl. Serve the soup sprinkled with the seeds.

It's ready!

Tip: This soup is energizing and is very good cold, but on winter evenings, you can heat it up very gently in a saucepan.

Shopping: You can find wakame seaweed powder in organic food stores or online.

GREEN
GAZPACHO

SERVES 4

PREPARATION TIME: 15 MINUTES

INGREDIENTS

2 CUCUMBERS, PEELED, SEEDED, AND CHOPPED

2 ZUCCHINI, PEELED AND CHOPPED

2 GREEN ONIONS, CHOPPED

½ GREEN BELL PEPPER, CHOPPED

JUICE OF 2 LIMES

¾-INCH (2-CM) PIECE OF GINGER, GRATED

2 TEASPOONS PEPITAS (PUMPKIN SEEDS)

2 TEASPOONS FLAXSEEDS

2 TEASPOONS BROWN MUSTARD SEEDS

1 AVOCADO

1 TABLESPOON CANOLA OIL

FLEUR DE SEL (FINE SEA SALT)

Preparing my soup

Purée the cucumbers, zucchini, green onions, and bell pepper with 1¼ cups (10 fl oz/300 ml) water, the lime juice, and the ginger until smooth. Strain, if necessary, and add a little more water, if needed. Set aside in the refrigerator. Mix the seeds together. Dice the avocado and serve in individual bowls with the soup. At the last moment, add a drizzle of canola oil and a sprinkling of sea salt, freshly ground pepper, and seeds on top.

It's ready!

Extra: For a more complete meal, add 2 oz (60 g) diced very fresh raw salmon.

QUICK PISTOU
SOUP

SERVES 4

PREPARATION TIME: 25 MINUTES

COOKING TIME: 20 MINUTES

INGREDIENTS

1 CELERY RIB, CHOPPED

6 OZ (170 G) GREEN BEANS, TRIMMED AND CUT
INTO SHORT LENGTHS

1 LARGE POTATO (SKIN ON IF ORGANIC),

CUT INTO LARGE CUBES

⅔ CUP (3½ OZ/100 G) SHELLED PEAS

1 QUART (32 FL OZ/1 LITER) HOT CHICKEN STOCK

1 FIRM ZUCCHINI (SKIN ON IF ORGANIC),
CUT INTO LARGE CUBES

1 HEAPING CUP (7 OZ/200 G) COOKED OR CANNED
WHITE BEANS

10 CHERRY TOMATOES, HALVED

½ BUNCH (2¼ OZ/60 G) BASIL

½ GARLIC CLOVE

3 TABLESPOONS (1 OZ/25 G) PINE NUTS

¼ CUP (1 OZ/25 G) GRATED PARMESAN CHEESE

2½ TABLESPOONS OLIVE OIL

Preparing my soup

Put the celery, green beans, potato, peas, and stock into a heavy stockpot. Cover, bring to a boil, reduce the heat to medium-low, and simmer very gently for 15 minutes. Add the zucchini, white beans, and tomatoes, and cook for a further 5 minutes. Meanwhile, in the bowl of a food processor, make the pesto by puréeing the basil leaves with the garlic, pine nuts, Parmesan, olive oil, and a little salt and pepper. Serve the soup very hot with 1 tablespoon pesto in each bowl.

It's ready!

Note from Delphine: I'm not a big fan of garlic, so I put in only half a clove, but you can always add more to taste.

PROSCIUTTO
& BEAN SALAD

Non-Fast Day

SERVES 4

PREPARATION TIME: 20 MINUTES

COOKING TIME: 15 MINUTES

INGREDIENTS

8 OZ (225 G) GREEN BEANS, TRIMMED

3 TABLESPOONS (1 OZ/25 G) PINE NUTS, TOASTED

2 GREEN ONIONS, SLICED

8 SLICES PROSCIUTTO, CUT INTO PIECES

½ BUNCH (1½ OZ/40 G) CILANTRO, CHOPPED

2 HANDFULS (1¾ OZ/50 G) MIXED SALAD LEAVES

1 SMALL TABLESPOON MAPLE SYRUP

2 TABLESPOONS OLIVE OIL

FLEUR DE SEL (FINE SEA SALT)

½ CUP (2¼ OZ/60 G) AGED MIMOLETTE OR PARMESAN CHEESE

Preparing my meal

Steam the green beans until just tender-crisp, about 10 minutes. Run them under cold water to stop the cooking. Drain and place in a salad bowl. Add the pine nuts, green onions, prosciutto, cilantro, and mixed salad leaves. Make a dressing by mixing the maple syrup with the olive oil, a little sea salt, and some pepper. At the last minute, dress the salad and finish with shavings of cheese, made with a vegetable peeler.

It's ready!

Extra: For a more complete meal, add one soft-boiled egg per person to the salad. (Cook for 5–6 minutes in boiling water, then peel it under cold running water.)

Variation: Replace the prosciutto with bresaola or other dried meat.

SQUASH SOUP

À L'ORANGE

Non-Fast Day

SERVES 4

PREPARATION TIME: 15 MINUTES

COOKING TIME: 25 MINUTES

INGREDIENTS

1 SMALL RED KURI (HOKKAIDO) SQUASH,
ABOUT 2½ LB (1.2 KG)

GRATED ZEST AND JUICE OF 1 ORGANIC ORANGE

1 BOUQUET GARNI: PARSLEY, THYME & BAY LEAF

FLEUR DE SEL (FINE SEA SALT)

OLIVE OIL

GLUTEN-FREE ◆

Preparing my soup

Wash and scrub the skin of the squash (if it's organic, leave the skin on—otherwise peel). Halve, seed, and cut into large cubes. Put into a large saucepan with the orange zest and juice, the bouquet garni, and a little sea salt and pepper. Cover with water and cook until the squash pieces are tender, about 25 minutes. Remove the squash from the broth, reserving the liquid. Purée the squash with a little broth and gradually thin it out, ladleful by ladleful, with additonal broth, until it's the consistency you like. Taste and adjust the seasoning and serve immediately, sprinkled with a few drops of olive oil.

It's ready!

Note from Delphine: I love sipping this soup when it's cold outside. I add chopped toasted hazelnuts and 2-3 tablespoons wild rice.

FENNEL
& ENDIVE SALAD

NON-
FAST
Day

SERVES 4
PREPARATION TIME: 20 MINUTES

INGREDIENTS

2 BELGIAN ENDIVES

2 SMALL FENNEL BULBS

½ PRESERVED LEMON

20 CAPERBERRIES, RINSED

6 FLAT-LEAF PARSLEY SPRIGS, CHOPPED

JUICE OF ½ LEMON

½ TEASPOON MUSTARD

½ TEASPOON CRÈME FRAÎCHE

½ TABLESPOON WHITE WINE VINEGAR

2 TABLESPOONS OLIVE OIL

2 TABLESPOONS CRUSHED ALMONDS

Preparing my meal

Discard the two or three outer leaves of the endive. Trim the bases and cut out the central core at the bottom to remove the bitterness. Slice into strips. Discard the hard outer layer of the fennel bulbs and thinly slice the fennel using a very sharp knife or a mandoline. Wash and drain the slices. Rinse the preserved lemon under cold running water and remove the seeds, then cut it into small pieces. Combine the fennel, endive, preserved lemon, caperberries, and parsley. Make a dressing by mixing together the lemon juice, mustard, crème fraîche, white wine vinegar, olive oil, and a little freshly ground pepper. Pour this over, then toss the salad to combine and keep in the refrigerator before serving. Serve with the crushed almonds scattered on top.

It's ready!

Extra: For a more substantial salad, add 1 cup (5 oz/150 g) drained and flaked tuna at the last moment.

ZUCCHINI
& PARMESAN

SERVES 4

PREPARATION TIME: 15 MINUTES

INGREDIENTS

1 TABLESPOON OLIVE OIL

1 TEASPOON PUMPKIN SEED OIL

1 TEASPOON HAZELNUT OIL

2 YELLOW SUMMER SQUASH
(OR 4 IF THEY ARE REALLY SMALL)

2 MINT SPRIGS, LEAVES PICKED

1 TABLESPOON CRUSHED TOASTED HAZELNUTS

½ CUP (2 OZ/60 G) PARMESAN CHEESE

GLUTEN-FREE ◆

Preparing my meal

Make a dressing by combining the oils with a little sea salt and freshly ground
pepper. Pour the dressing over the base of a large plate (where you'll lay out
the squash when it's sliced). Slice the squash very thinly using a very sharp
knife or a mandoline. Arrange on the plate and top with the mint leaves
and hazelnuts. Grate the Parmesan over the top and serve immediately.

It's ready!

Variation 1: Replace the Parmesan with pecorino cheese.

Variation 2: Replace the pumpkin seed oil and hazelnut oil
with just olive oil. Use a little less than 2 tablespoons in total.

Extra: For a substantial salad to have for lunch, add mozzarella and thin
slices of finely shredded prosciutto.

Shopping: You can find pumpkin seed oil in organic food stores or online.

SWEET SALAD

SERVES 4
PREPARATION TIME: 20 MINUTES

INGREDIENTS
¾-INCH (2-CM) PIECE OF GINGER, GRATED
1 SHALLOT, CHOPPED
1 TABLESPOON RICE VINEGAR
1 TABLESPOON VEGETABLE OIL
½ TEASPOON SOY SAUCE
½ TEASPOON FISH SAUCE
JUICE OF ½ LIME
1 MANGO, RIPE BUT STILL FAIRLY FIRM, PEELED AND DICED
10 OZ (300 G) CARROTS, GRATED
2 LARGE HANDFULS (1 OZ/30 G) CILANTRO LEAVES, CHOPPED
10 MINT LEAVES

Preparing my meal
Make a dressing by mixing together the ginger, shallot, vinegar, oil, soy sauce, fish sauce, lime juice, and pepper. Mix together the mango, carrots, and herbs and drizzle with the dressing. Taste and adjust the salt and pepper if necessary.

It's ready!

ASPARAGUS,

ZUCCHINI & FETA SALAD

SERVES 4
PREPARATION TIME: 15 MINUTES
COOKING TIME: 10 MINUTES

INGREDIENTS

14 OZ (400 G) ASPARAGUS, TRIMMED

1⅓ CUPS (7¼ OZ/205 G) SHELLED PEAS

2 SMALL, FIRM ZUCCHINI, SLICED INTO THIN ROUNDS

⅔ CUP (3½ OZ/100 G) CRUMBLED FETA CHEESE

25 G (1 OZ/1 LARGE HANDFUL) ARUGULA

1 TABLESPOON TOASTED SESAME SEEDS

GRATED ZEST OF 1 ORGANIC LEMON

1–2 TABLESPOONS OLIVE OIL

GLUTEN-FREE ◆

NON-
FAST
Day

Preparing my meal

Cook the asparagus and peas in salted boiling water for 10 minutes, then immerse in a bowl of iced water to stop the cooking. Drain and pat dry with paper towels. Combine the asparagus, peas, zucchini, feta, arugula, sesame seeds, and lemon zest in a bowl or on a serving plate. Sprinkle with the olive oil, season with salt and pepper, and serve immediately.

It's ready!

Extra: Add chicken breasts, browned in a frying pan. First, marinate them in 1 tablespoon olive oil, 2 tablespoons lemon juice, 1 tablespoon agave syrup, and ½ teaspoon ground cumin. Cook over high heat for 3 minutes on each side, then over low heat, covered, for 5 minutes.

SPICY CHICKPEA
SALAD

Non-
Fast
Day

SERVES 4

PREPARATION TIME: 20 MINUTES

COOKING TIME: 2 MINUTES

INGREDIENTS

3 OZ (90 G) SPANISH-STYLE FIRM CHORIZO
(ABOUT 1½ SAUSAGES), THINLY SLICED

2 TEASPOONS WHITE WINE VINEGAR

1 TEASPOON HOT MUSTARD

2 TABLESPOONS OLIVE OIL

FLEUR DE SEL (FINE SEA SALT)

2½ CUPS (14 OZ/400 G) COOKED OR CANNED CHICKPEAS,
RINSED AND DRAINED

1 AVOCADO, DICED

2 GREEN ONIONS, THINLY SLICED

5 FLAT-LEAF PARSLEY SPRIGS

2 TARRAGON SPRIGS

GRATED ZEST OF 1 ORGANIC LIME

Preparing my meal

Brown the chorizo slices in a medium frying pan over medium heat on
both sides for 1–2 minutes. Drain on paper towels. In a salad bowl, make
a dressing from the white wine vinegar, mustard, olive oil, a little sea salt
and lots of pepper. Add the chickpeas, avocado, green onions, parsley,
tarragon, and chorizo. Mix together well and sprinkle with the lime zest.

It's ready!

SUPER
TABBOULEH

SERVES 4
PREPARATION TIME: 25 MINUTES
COOKING TIME: 10 MINUTES
REFRIGERATION TIME: 3 HOURS

NON-FAST Day

INGREDIENTS

JUICE OF 1 LEMON
1 TABLESPOON CANOLA OIL
1 TABLESPOON HAZELNUT OIL
FLEUR DE SEL (FINE SEA SALT)
8 OZ (225 G) ASPARAGUS
½ CAULIFLOWER
1 SMALL CUCUMBER, PEELED IF DESIRED
8 CHERRY TOMATOES
2 GREEN ONIONS
⅓ CUP (2¼ OZ/60 G) WHOLE-WHEAT INSTANT COUSCOUS, COOKED (SEE EXTRA, PAGE 190)
4 MINT SPRIGS, CHOPPED
4 FLAT-LEAF PARSLEY SPRIGS, CHOPPED

Preparing my meal

In a large bowl, combine the lemon juice with the oils, a little sea salt, and two or three turns of the pepper mill. Prepare the asparagus: trim the bases, then peel the spears without touching the tips. Steam for about 10 minutes. Check whether they're ready with the tip of a knife: they should still be a little firm. Let cool on paper towels. Cut up the cauliflower and keep only the small florets (cut off all the stems). Using a mandoline, grate the florets to make little grains of cauliflower, and set these aside. Halve and seed the cucumber and cut it into small cubes. Cut the tomatoes into wedges. Chop the green onions and cut the asparagus into short lengths. Add all the ingredients to the dressing in the bowl, including the couscous and chopped herbs. Mix together well and refrigerate for at least 3 hours, stirring occasionally. Before serving, taste and adjust the seasoning.

It's ready!

Tip: To stop the herbs from being "cooked" by the dressing (because of the lemon juice), you can also chop and mix them in at the last minute before serving.

WARM LENTIL SALAD

& HEIRLOOM VEGETABLES

Non-Fast Day

SERVES 4

PREPARATION TIME: 20 MINUTES

COOKING TIME: 32 MINUTES

INGREDIENTS

¾ CUP (5½ OZ/150 G) FRENCH LENTILS

2 OZ (60 G) SMOKED BACON, CHOPPED

1 SMALL PARSNIP, CUT INTO STICKS

1 CUP (5½ OZ/150 G) CUBED BUTTERNUT SQUASH

1 TABLESPOON FLAXSEEDS

3 TABLESPOONS (1 OZ/25 G) SUNFLOWER SEED KERNELS, TOASTED

3 TABLESPOONS (1 OZ/25 G) PINE NUTS, TOASTED

1 TABLESPOON BALSAMIC GLAZE

2 TABLESPOONS ORANGE JUICE

2 TABLESPOONS OLIVE OIL

FLEUR DE SEL (FINE SEA SALT)

Preparing my meal

In a saucepan, cover the lentils with water and cook for 25 minutes in total, including the time they take to come to a boil. The lentils should be al dente. Set aside. Drop the bacon into boiling water for 1 minute, drain, and place on paper towels. Heat a large frying pan over high heat and add the chopped bacon. Add the parsnip and squash and brown for 2–3 minutes. Stir with a wooden spoon, reduce the heat slightly, and cook for 3–4 minutes. Roughly crush the seeds and pine nuts. Make a vinaigrette by mixing the balsamic glaze, orange juice, and olive oil, and seasoning with sea salt and pepper. Combine the lentils with the parsnip, squash, and seed and nut mixture; add the dressing, taste, and adjust the seasoning.

It's ready!

Extra: Cook two duck breasts in a hot frying pan, 7 minutes on the skin side and 3 minutes on the flesh side. Drain, allow to cool until just warm, and slice thinly before serving with the salad.

Classic version: Replace the parsnip with carrots and choose other winter squash beside butternut.

CREAM OF LENTIL SOUP
WITH HADDOCK

SERVES 4

PREPARATION TIME: 20 MINUTES

SOAKING TIME: OVERNIGHT

COOKING TIME: 30 MINUTES

INGREDIENTS

8 OZ (225 G) SMOKED HADDOCK

1 QUART (32 FL OZ/1 LITER) MILK

1 CUP (7 OZ/200 G) FRENCH LENTILS

2 SHALLOTS, CHOPPED

½ LEEK, PALE PART ONLY, CHOPPED

1 SMALL CARROT, CHOPPED

½ CUP (4 FL OZ/125 ML) LIGHT CREAM

¼ CUP (2 FL OZ/50 ML) WHITE WINE

300 ML (10½ FL OZ) HOT CHICKEN STOCK

1 TABLESPOON SESAME SEEDS, TOASTED

Preparing my soup

Soak the haddock for several hours or overnight in the milk. In a large saucepan, cook the lentils with the shallots, leek, and carrot in a large quantity of water seasoned with salt and pepper for 30 minutes. Put the vegetables and their cooking liquid through a food mill. Transfer the mixture to a blender and add the cream and white wine. Blend, check the texture, and gradually add the stock, little by little, until the soup is the consistency you want. Add a little pepper if necessary, but don't add salt because the haddock is already salty enough. Reheat very gently in a saucepan before serving. Drain the haddock, wipe it dry and cut it into small cubes (without the skin). Serve the soup nice and hot with the cubes of haddock on top and sprinkled with sesame seeds.

It's ready!

Note from Delphine: I really like the consistency of this soup when it's thick, and I enjoy it as a main course on chilly winter evenings.

Variation: Replace the haddock with very fresh raw salmon.

SMOKED MACKEREL
& ROASTED BUCKWHEAT

NON-
FAST
Day

SERVES 4

PREPARATION TIME: 20 MINUTES

COOKING TIME: 7 MINUTES

INGREDIENTS

1¾ CUPS (10 OZ/300 G) ROASTED BUCKWHEAT (KASHA)

1 TABLESPOON CANOLA OIL

JUICE OF ½ LIME

FLEUR DE SEL (FINE SEA SALT)

10 OZ (300 G) BUTTERNUT SQUASH

2 TABLESPOONS OLIVE OIL

4 SMOKED MACKEREL FILLETS WITH CRUSHED PEPPERCORNS, SKIN REMOVED AND FLAKED

1 HANDFUL (1 OZ/25 G) BABY SPINACH

4 CHERVIL SPRIGS, CHOPPED

GLUTEN-FREE ♦

Preparing my meal

Pour the buckwheat into a medium saucepan of boiling water and cook for 3–4 minutes. Taste: it should stay a little crunchy. Drain and pour the buckwheat into a salad bowl, dress with the canola oil and lime juice, and season with sea salt and pepper. Halve and seed the squash, remove the skin, and cut the flesh into small cubes. Heat a few drops of olive oil in a frying pan, add the cubes of squash, and brown over high heat for 2–3 minutes. Add the squash to the bowl along with the mackerel, baby spinach, and chervil. Dress with the remaining olive oil and a little sea salt, stir, taste, and adjust the seasoning if necessary.

It's ready!

Tip: You can warm up the mackerel for a few seconds before serving…it tastes even better!

Shopping: You can find smoked mackerel with crushed peppercorns in the refrigerated section of well-stocked supermarkets, organic food stores, or online. If you need a substitute, try another fatty, flaky-textured fish, such as herring or trout.

POT LUCK SALAD
WITH SMOKED MACKEREL

NON-FAST *Day*

SERVES 4

PREPARATION TIME: 20 MINUTES

COOKING TIME: 1½ HOURS

INGREDIENTS

½ CUP (3½ OZ/100 G) WHOLE BLACK RICE

1½ CUPS (9½ OZ/270 G) COOKED OR CANNED KIDNEY BEANS (SEE PAGE 124)

1 SMALL FIRM ZUCCHINI, DICED

1 SMALL ONION, SLICED

GRATED ZEST OF 1 ORGANIC LIME

16 CHERRY TOMATOES, ABOUT 7 OZ (200 G), QUARTERED

1 PERSIAN CUCUMBER, PEELED AND CUBED

1 AVOCADO, COARSELY CHOPPED

1 TABLESPOON MIXED SEEDS (SUNFLOWER, SESAME…)

A FEW TARRAGON LEAVES

1 TABLESPOON OLIVE OIL

1 TABLESPOON PUMPKIN SEED OIL

1 TABLESPOON WHITE OR DARK BALSAMIC GLAZE

4 SMOKED MACKEREL FILLETS WITH CRUSHED PEPPERCORNS (OR OTHER FATTY, FLAKY-TEXTURED FISH SUCH AS TROUT)

GLUTEN-FREE ◆

Preparing my meal

Cook the black rice following the instructions on page 124. Rinse beans and combine with the rice in a large mixing bowl to let cool. Add the zucchini, onion, lime zest, tomatoes, cucumber, avocado, seeds, and tarragon leaves. Make a dressing with the olive oil, pumpkin seed oil, balsamic glaze, and salt and a little pepper. Pour over the vegetables and mix together. Remove the skin from the mackerel fillets and serve them with the salad.

It's ready!

Tip: Add any seasonal vegetables to this salad, chopped into small pieces, even raw (Jerusalem artichokes, radish, carrots, celery, turnips, asparagus, mushrooms…).

Delphine's advice: If you don't like whole black rice, replace it with basmati rice (its glycemic index is higher…but it is also very good!).

Shopping: You can find pumpkin seed oil, seeds, and mackerel fillets in organic food stores or online.

Note from Delphine: Ever since I discovered the mackerel fillets in the refrigerated aisle of my organic food store, I've been buying them all the time. You can warm them up for a few seconds in a saucepan of hot water, still in their packaging. They taste even better that way! I often cook my grains, beans, and quinoa in large quantities that I keep in a pretty covered ceramic dish in the refrigerator for several days.

FISH
TARTARE

SERVES 4

PREPARATION TIME: 20 MINUTES

COOKING TIME: 20 MINUTES

INGREDIENTS

½ CUP (3 OZ/95 G) FRENCH LENTILS

14 OZ (400 G) VERY FRESH RAW POLLACK
(ALTERNATIVELY, USE COD)

1 GREEN ONION, THINLY SLICED

¾ OZ (20 G) SPANISH-STYLE FIRM CHORIZO
(ABOUT ⅓ OF A SAUSAGE), DICED

1 LARGE HANDFUL (1 OZ/25 G) ARUGULA

2 TARRAGON SPRIGS, LEAVES PICKED

2 TABLESPOONS OLIVE OIL

FLEUR DE SEL (FINE SEA SALT)

Preparing my meal

Rinse the lentils, put them in a medium saucepan with three times their volume of water, and cook them over medium heat for 20 minutes. Drain and let cool. Clean the pieces of fish, wipe them dry, and cut into small cubes. Combine the fish with the green onion, chorizo, arugula, lentils, and tarragon leaves. Dress with the olive oil and sprinkle lightly with sea salt. Toss and serve at room temperature, or refrigerate to eat cold a little later.

It's ready!

Tip: Serve this dish as a main meal—it's quite substantial!

Variation: Replace the chorizo with 4 slices of prosciutto or bresaola.

SALMON CHIRASHI
REVISITED

NON-FAST Day

SERVES 4
PREPARATION TIME: 20 MINUTES
COOKING TIME: 20 MINUTES

INGREDIENTS

¾ CUP (5½ OZ/150 G) SUSHI RICE
2 TABLESPOONS RICE VINEGAR
8 OZ (225 G) VERY FRESH RAW SALMON
FLEUR DE SEL (FINE SEA SALT)
1 AVOCADO
JUICE OF ½ LIME
½-INCH (1-CM) PIECE OF GINGER, CHOPPED
1 TABLESPOON SOY SAUCE
1 TABLESPOON OLIVE OIL
1 TEASPOON SESAME OIL
1 TEASPOON BLACK SESAME SEEDS
8 CILANTRO SPRIGS, CHOPPED

Preparing my meal

Cook the rice following the instructions on the packet, drain, sprinkle with the rice vinegar, and allow to cool. Rinse the salmon, pat dry, and cut into small cubes. Season the salmon with sea salt and freshly ground pepper and set aside. Thinly slice the avocado and sprinkle with the lime juice so it doesn't oxidize. Make a dressing with the ginger, soy sauce, olive oil, sesame oil, and a little pepper. Place the rice in the bottom of four serving dishes, top with the avocado, then the salmon. Dress with the sauce and sprinkle with sesame seeds and cilantro.

It's ready!

Extra: Replace the sushi rice with a glutinous rice to serve hot as a side to the salmon, with avocado served as a salad. Wash the rice until the water runs clear. Cover with water and soak for 12 hours (overnight) in the refrigerator. Drain and steam for 1 hour. The rice is cooked when it's translucent and perfectly sticky.

Variation: You can replace the salmon with very fresh raw sea bream or tuna, or large cooked shrimp.

Shopping: You can find black sesame seeds in organic food stores; alternatively, use standard sesame seeds, lightly toasted in a frying pan.

FISH
& PEAS

NON-
FAST
Day

SERVES 4

PREPARATION TIME: 10 MINUTES

COOKING TIME: 23 MINUTES

INGREDIENTS

2¾ CUPS (14 OZ/400 G) SHELLED PEAS
(2 LB/1 KG IN THEIR PODS)

8 CHERRY TOMATOES

2¼ OZ (60 G) SPANISH-STYLE FIRM CHORIZO
(1 SAUSAGE), DICED

2 SHALLOTS, CHOPPED

4 SEA BREAM FILLETS, OR OTHER FIRM WHITE FISH

3 BASIL SPRIGS, LEAVES PICKED

FLEUR DE SEL (FINE SEA SALT)

Preparing my meal

Steam the peas and tomatoes for 10 minutes. Sauté the diced chorizo with the shallots in a frying pan over medium heat for 3 minutes. Drain on paper towels. Leave the frying pan on the heat and add the fish fillets to the pan. Cook over medium heat for 2 minutes on each side, then over low heat for 2 minutes on each side with the pan covered. Still over low heat, add the peas and tomatoes, chorizo, and shallots and cook for a further 2 minutes. Check that the fish is cooked through, season with a little sea salt and freshly ground pepper, and serve immediately with the basil scattered over.

It's ready!

Extra: Serve with whole-wheat instant couscous. Allow ⅓ cup (1¾ oz/50 g) per person. Pour one part boiling salted water (with two or three drops of olive oil) over one part couscous. Let stand, covered, for 7 minutes, then fluff up with a fork.

GRILLED FISH
& VEGETABLE MASH

Non-Fast Day

SERVES 4

PREPARATION TIME: 20 MINUTES

COOKING TIME: 25 MINUTES

INGREDIENTS

8 BABY RED MULLET FILLETS
(ALTERNATIVELY, USE SEA BASS OR OCEAN PERCH)

14 OZ (400 G) POTATOES

2 ZUCCHINI

1 TEASPOON OLIVE OIL

1 CUP (2 OZ/60 G) DRY SUN-DRIED TOMATOES,
PLUMPED IN WARM WATER AND CHOPPED

4 BASIL SPRIGS, CHOPPED

3 TABLESPOONS (¾ OZ/20 G) PARMESAN
CHEESE SHAVINGS

A FEW MINT LEAVES

FLEUR DE SEL (FINE SEA SALT)

GLUTEN-FREE ◆

Preparing my meal

Ask the fishmonger to prepare the red mullet fillets and make sure all the bones are removed. Peel the potatoes and zucchini (you can leave the skin on organic zucchini), cut into chunks, and steam for 20 minutes. Put them in a bowl with the olive oil, season with salt and pepper, and crush them all together to make a lovely mash. Keep some solid pieces or not, according to taste. Mix in the sun-dried tomatoes and basil. Rinse the mullet fillets and pat dry. Place a large sheet of baking parchment in a heavy frying pan (or on a hotplate!). Add a drop of olive oil and, once the pan is quite hot, lay down the fillets skin side down (in batches if necessary) and let them sear for 2–3 minutes. Reduce the heat, cover, and cook for a further 2 minutes. Serve immediately with the mash, sprinkled with the Parmesan shavings, mint, and sea salt and pepper.

It's ready!

THE CLUB SANDWICH

Non-Fast Day

SERVES 4

PREPARATION TIME: 10 MINUTES

INGREDIENTS

1 SMALL AVOCADO

JUICE OF ½ LIME

8 SLICES WHOLE-GRAIN BREAD, CRUSTS REMOVED

10 CHIVES, SNIPPED

10 CILANTRO SPRIGS, COARSELY CHOPPED

6 OZ (180 G) TOMATOES, SLICED INTO ROUNDS

6 OZ (180 G) BONELESS, SKINLESS CHICKEN BREAST, COOKED AND THINLY SLICED (SEE EXTRA, PAGE 161)

4 LETTUCE LEAVES

Preparing my meal

Mash the avocado flesh with the lime juice, and season with salt and pepper. Toast the bread. Spread the mashed avocado on all the slices. Divide the herbs among four of the slices, then the tomatoes and chicken, and finish with a lettuce leaf. Place the remaining four slices of bread on top. Using a sharp knife, trim off any filling that's poking out the side and cut each sandwich in two for easier eating.

It's ready!

BEEF CARPACCIO

NON-FAST Day

SERVES 4

PREPARATION TIME: 20 MINUTES

FREEZING TIME: 2 HOURS

INGREDIENTS

14 OZ (400 G) VERY FRESH RAW BEEF TENDERLOIN OR SIRLOIN

½ FENNEL BULB

4 ASPARAGUS SPEARS

2 GREEN ONIONS

1 LARGE HANDFUL (1 OZ/25 G) ARUGULA

8 BLACK OLIVES, PITTED

2½ TABLESPOONS OLIVE OIL

FLEUR DE SEL (FINE SEA SALT)

10 SMALL MUSHROOMS, BRUSHED

GLUTEN-FREE ◆

Preparing my meal

Wrap the piece of beef in plastic wrap and place in the freezer for 2 hours. Discard the tough outer layer of the fennel bulb and slice the fennel thinly, preferably with a mandoline. Peel and chop the asparagus into rounds, and set aside the tips. Slice the green onions thinly from top to bottom. Spin dry the arugula, if needed. Put the asparagus tips and pitted olives in the bowl of a food processor, add the olive oil and a little salt and pepper, and pulse the mixture a few times. Set aside. Take the piece of beef out of the freezer, remove the plastic wrap, and slice the beef very thinly using a very sharp knife. Lay the slices on four chilled plates as you go. Dress with the sauce and garnish with the fennel, asparagus, and green onions. At the last minute, thinly slice the mushrooms over each plate using a mandoline, and add the arugula.

It's ready!

Extra: Serve with black rice (see page 124) and a little mozzarella.

Special treat variation: Serve with a portion of oven-baked fries (fewer calories) or homemade mashed potato (use potatoes that have boiled or steamed for 20 minutes, then mash them with a fork with a little butter, olive oil, and salt and pepper).

Note from Delphine: It's not essential to have all the vegetables. I use what I have in my refrigerator, and sometimes I even ask my butcher to slice some carpaccio directly onto my plates! I also often add some Parmesan cheese. It's so good, but I grate it very finely, which means I use less.

THE SUNDAY ROAST
CHICKEN

Non- Fast Day

SERVES 4

PREPARATION TIME: 10 MINUTES

COOKING TIME: 1½ HOURS

INGREDIENTS

1 FREE-RANGE CHICKEN, ABOUT 3 LB (1.5 KG)

1 TUB (1 OZ/30 G) PETIT-SUISSE CHEESE
(ALTERNATIVELY, USE RICOTTA)

1¼-INCH (3-CM) PIECE OF GINGER, SLICED

1 ORGANIC LEMON, HALVED

OLIVE OIL

1 TABLESPOON (½ OZ/15 G) BUTTER

1 ONION, SLICED

1 VINE BRANCH OF CHERRY TOMATOES, PICKED

GLUTEN-FREE ◆

Preparing my meal

Preheat the oven to 400°F (200°C). Season the inside of the chicken with salt and pepper and empty the tub of petit-suisse inside the cavity with the sliced ginger and half the lemon (chopped). Put the chicken in a baking dish, coat it with olive oil, and dot with pieces of the butter. Put the chicken in the oven and roast, basting regularly with its juices. After 45 minutes, arrange the onion, tomatoes, and the rest of the lemon (chopped) around the chicken. Cook for another 45 minutes.

It's ready!

Delphine's advice: Enjoy a beautiful chicken breast with the onions, tomatoes, and lemon, but leave the fatty juices and mashed potatoes to the others. Serve with a lovely green salad with herbs.

POT-AU-FEU

NON-
FAST
Day

SERVES 4

PREPARATION TIME: 20 MINUTES

COOKING TIME: 3½ HOURS

INGREDIENTS

1½ LB (700 G) BRAISING BEEF (CHUCK, BLADE,
SHANK), FAIRLY LEAN

3 CARROTS, QUARTERED LENGTHWISE

2 SHALLOTS, PEELED AND LEFT WHOLE

1 GARLIC CLOVE, PEELED AND LEFT WHOLE

1¼-INCH (3-CM) PIECE OF GINGER, THINLY SLICED

1 SMALL RED CHILE

6 KAFFIR LIME LEAVES OR 2 LEMONGRASS STALKS

1 TABLESPOON SOY SAUCE

1 TEASPOON PEPPERCORNS

1 TEASPOON COARSE SALT

8 CILANTRO SPRIGS,
LEAVES AND STEMS CHOPPED

4 THAI EGGPLANTS OR 1 MEDIUM
EGGPLANT, CUT INTO CHUNKS

1 HANDFUL BEAN SPROUTS

1 MINT SPRIG, LEAVES PICKED

1 LIME

Preparing my meal

Rinse the meat under cold water. Submerge it in a large flameproof casserole dish full of water and bring to a boil on the stove top. Skim for as long as foam rises, then drain the pot and rinse the meat. Preheat the oven to 275°F (140°C). Return the meat to the casserole dish, add the carrots, shallots, garlic, ginger, chile, lime leaves (if using lemongrass stalks, discard the outer layer of the lemongrass stalk, trim the base, and cut the more tender part into short lengths), soy sauce, peppercorns, coarse salt, and cilantro (leaves and stems). Add enough water to just cover the meat and bring to a boil. Cover with the lid and braise in the oven for 2 hours. Add the eggplant to the casserole dish and cook for a further 45 minutes. Add the bean sprouts and cook for a further 15 minutes. Discard the lemongrass, if using, and cilantro. Serve the beef very hot, garnished with mint leaves and accompanied with the vegetables and broth. Add a little lime wedge to each plate.

It's ready!

Extra: For a bun bo version, add rice vermicelli to the broth 5 minutes before the end of the cooking time.

Tip: I love making this pot-au-feu ahead of time for nights when it's very cold outside. When there's leftover broth, I use it for a Fast Day with a big handful of bean sprouts, a few grated vegetables, and 2 oz (60 g) beef tenderloin, chopped up tartare-style.

THAI-STYLE
PORK

SERVES 4

PREPARATION TIME: 25 MINUTES

COOKING TIME: 2½ HOURS

REFRIGERATION TIME: A FEW HOURS

OR OVERNIGHT (OPTIONAL)

INGREDIENTS

2 LB (1 KG) PORK SHOULDER, CUT INTO PIECES

4 KAFFIR LIME LEAVES

2 LARGE HANDFULS (1 OZ/30 G) CILANTRO LEAVES, CHOPPED

2 MINT SPRIGS, CHOPPED

1 GARLIC CLOVE

3 SHALLOTS, CUT INTO WEDGES

1 SMALL RED CHILE

1¼-INCH (3-CM) PIECE OF GINGER, GRATED

1 TABLESPOON SOY SAUCE

1⅓ CUPS (9 OZ/250 G) BROWN JASMINE RICE

2 FENNEL BULBS

⅔ CUP (5 FL OZ/150 ML) COCONUT MILK

1 TEASPOON OLIVE OIL

Preparing my meal

Preheat the oven to 350°F (180°C). Put the pork in a flameproof casserole dish with the lime leaves, half the cilantro, half the mint, the garlic, shallots, chile, ginger, and soy sauce. Cover with water just to the top of the meat and bring to a boil on the stove top. Cover the casserole dish and braise in the oven for 2 hours. Set the meat aside, reserving the cooking broth. Cook the rice following the instructions on the packet. Trim the fennel bulbs, discard the hard outer layer, cut the bulbs into thick wedges, and steam them for 15 minutes. Add the coconut milk to the broth once the fat has been skimmed (see tip below). Boil for 10 minutes, then add the meat and reheat very gently. Place the fennel wedges in a large ovenproof dish, sprinkle the olive oil over, stir, and place under the broiler for 5–10 minutes so they're well browned. Remove the meat from the broth and serve in deep plates. Scatter the rest of the cilantro and the fresh mint over the meat and rice. Serve the pork accompanied with the rice mixed with the fennel, and the broth on the side.

It's ready!

Tip: If you have time, make this dish the day before so you can skim the fat. It's better for your figure, after all! In that case, take the meat out and leave it in a large dish in the refrigerator. Refrigerate the broth overnight or for a few hours so you can easily remove the layer of fat that will form on top.

SQUASH, LAMB
& CHICKPEA TAGINE

NON-
FAST
Day

SERVES 4

PREPARATION TIME: 25 MINUTES

COOKING TIME: 2¼ HOURS

INGREDIENTS

2 LB (1 KG) LAMB SHOULDER, CUT INTO LARGE PIECES
AND PATTED DRY

1 TABLESPOON OLIVE OIL

2 ONIONS, SLICED

¾-INCH (2-CM) PIECE OF GINGER, GRATED

1 GARLIC CLOVE, CHOPPED

1 PRESERVED LEMON, RINSED, SEEDED,
AND FINELY CHOPPED

FLEUR DE SEL (FINE SEA SALT)

1 PINCH SAFFRON

2 CUPS (16 FL OZ/500 ML) CHICKEN STOCK

½ RED KURI (HOKKAIDO) SQUASH

1¼ CUPS (7 OZ/200 G) COOKED OR CANNED CHICKPEAS,
RINSED AND DRAINED

2 TABLESPOONS CRUSHED TOASTED HAZELNUTS

2 MINT SPRIGS, LEAVES PICKED

Preparing my meal

Brown the meat with half the olive oil in a flameproof casserole dish over medium-high heat, in several batches if necessary. The dish should be very hot so the meat won't stew. Remove the meat, raise the heat to high, add the remaining olive oil and the onions, and sauté for 3 minutes. Reduce the heat, add the ginger, garlic, preserved lemon, and a little sea salt and pepper. Blend the saffron into the stock and add it to the dish. Bring to a boil, return the meat to the dish, reduce the heat to the lowest setting, cover, and braise for 2 hours. Meanwhile, halve and seed the squash, remove the skin if it is not organic, and cut the flesh into cubes. Add the squash cubes to the casserole 20 minutes before the end of the cooking time and the cooked chickpeas 10 minutes before the end. Check throughout the cooking time that there's enough liquid in the dish and add a little water if necessary. Check that the vegetables are cooked through (cook for a few more minutes if necessary). Serve sprinkled with the hazelnuts and mint.

It's ready!

Extra: Serve with whole-wheat instant couscous. Allow ⅓ cup (1¾ oz/50 g) per person. Pour one part boiling salted water (with two or three drops of olive oil) over one part couscous. Let stand, covered, for 7 minutes, then fluff up with a fork.

THAI DUCK BREAST
& CELLOPHANE NOODLES

NON-
FAST
Day

SERVES 4

PREPARATION TIME: 15 MINUTES

MARINATING TIME: 1 HOUR

COOKING TIME: 12 MINUTES

INGREDIENTS

2 TABLESPOONS SOY SAUCE

2 TABLESPOONS RICE VINEGAR

GRATED ZEST AND JUICE OF 1 ORGANIC LIME

¾-INCH (2-CM) PIECE OF GINGER, CUT INTO
THIN MATCHSTICKS

2 DUCK BREASTS

6 OZ (180 G) CELLOPHANE NOODLES

2 GREEN ONIONS, THINLY SLICED

2 LARGE HANDFULS (1 OZ/30 G) CILANTRO LEAVES,
CHOPPED

1 TABLESPOON PEANUTS, CHOPPED

Preparing my meal

Make a marinade with the soy sauce, rice vinegar, lime zest and juice, and the ginger matchsticks. Season lightly with pepper. Score the duck skin and pour the marinade over. Refrigerate for 1 hour, turning the breasts from time to time. Preheat the oven to 475°F (240°C). Drain the duck breasts, place them in a baking dish skin side up, and roast for 10 minutes. Wrap them in foil to keep warm and discard the fatty pan juices. Cook the noodles following the instructions on the packet. Boil the marinade for 2 minutes, then combine with the noodles and green onions. Serve the duck sliced, garnished with cilantro and peanuts, and accompanied with the noodles.

It's ready!

Tip: For breasts that are less pink, increase the cooking time by 3 minutes so they're more well done.

Note from Delphine: I cook the duck on a rack with a dish underneath to catch the fat and I throw it away. That way, my duck breasts aren't swimming in fat!

GRILLED CHICKEN
& CRUNCHY SALAD

NON-
Fast
Day

SERVES 4

PREPARATION TIME: 25 MINUTES

COOKING TIME: 11 MINUTES

MARINATING TIME: 1 HOUR

INGREDIENTS

3 TABLESPOONS OLIVE OIL

1 TABLESPOON MAPLE SYRUP

1 PINCH CHILI POWDER

4 BONELESS, SKINLESS CHICKEN BREASTS, ABOUT 4 OZ (125 G) EACH

1 AVOCADO

JUICE OF ½ LEMON

3 OZ (85 G) BABY SPINACH

⅓ BLACK RADISH (ALTERNATIVELY, USE TURNIP OR RUTABAGA)

2 COOKED ARTICHOKE HEARTS, CUT INTO SMALL PIECES

1 TABLESPOON SESAME OIL

1 TABLESPOON MIRIN

1 TEASPOON SOY SAUCE

1 TEASPOON RICE VINEGAR

1 SMALL RED CHILE, SEEDED AND CHOPPED

1 TEASPOON NIGELLA SEEDS

Preparing my meal

Make a marinade by mixing 2 tablespoons of the olive oil, the maple syrup, and the chili powder. Put the chicken breasts in the marinade and leave them in the refrigerator for 1 hour. Thinly slice the avocado and sprinkle it with the lemon juice so it doesn't oxidize. Spin the baby spinach dry, if needed, and peel and thinly slice the radish into slivers (this is very easy using a mandoline). Place all the vegetables in a mixing bowl and set aside. Heat a frying pan and sear the chicken breasts for 3 minutes over high heat; cover the pan, reduce the heat, and continue cooking gently for 5 minutes. Let the chicken breasts cool to lukewarm and slice them thinly. Make a sauce by combining the sesame oil, the remaining olive oil, the mirin, soy sauce, rice vinegar, chile, and a little salt and pepper. Pour the sauce over the salad, toss, and serve with the chicken slices sprinkled with nigella seeds.

It's ready!

Shopping: Buy nigella seeds in organic food stores. If you can't find them, you can replace them with sesame and/or sunflower seeds.

Variation: Replace the chicken with salmon fillets. Marinate them and cook in a hot frying pan for 2 minutes on each side. Wrap them in plastic wrap and refrigerate so they slice more easily, or serve as a whole fillet warm or even hot.

Warning: Go easy on the chile if you have a low tolerance!

VEAL TENDERLOIN

& LOTS OF GRILLED VEGETABLES

Non-Fast Day

SERVES 4

PREPARATION TIME: 20 MINUTES

COOKING TIME: 1 HOUR

INGREDIENTS

8 OZ (225 G) NEW OR CREAMER POTATOES

1 FIRM ZUCCHINI

1 SMALL BEET

4 SMALL TURNIPS

1 FENNEL BULB

½ PRESERVED LEMON, RINSED

¾-INCH (2-CM) PIECE OF GINGER, GRATED

2 TEASPOONS OLIVE OIL, PLUS EXTRA FOR DRIZZLING

1 TEASPOON (⅛ OZ/5 G) BUTTER

1 LB (500 G) VEAL TENDERLOIN, CUT INTO 8 PIECES

3 CHERVIL SPRIGS, CHOPPED

GLUTEN-FREE ◆

Preparing my meal

Preheat the oven to 400°F (200°C). Peel the potatoes, zucchini, beet, and turnips if they're not organic—otherwise, leave the skin on. Discard the fennel's tough outer layer. Cut up the vegetables (the fennel into wedges; the potatoes, zucchini, and beet into large cubes; the turnips in half). Remove the seeds from the preserved lemon and chop finely. Place all the vegetables in a large dish with the preserved lemon and ginger, drizzle with the extra olive oil, and season with salt and pepper. Bake for 1 hour, turning occasionally. For extra browning, place the vegetables under a broiler for 2–3 minutes before the end of the cooking time. Just before serving, heat the butter and 2 teaspoons olive oil in a large frying pan. As soon as it's quite hot, add the pieces of veal. Wait until the pieces of meat turn "white" two-thirds of the way up, then baste them with the melted butter. Turn off the heat, turn over the pieces of meat, and let rest for 3 minutes before serving with the vegetables. Sprinkle with chopped chervil and season the meat with salt and pepper at the table.

It's ready!

Light tip: You can also sear the meat without the oil and butter.

EXPRESS
JUICE!

MAKES 4 GLASSES
PREPARATION TIME: 5 MINUTES

INGREDIENTS
4 ORANGES
8 CARROTS, WELL WASHED,
PEELED IF NOT ORGANIC
1½-INCH (4-CM) PIECE OF GINGER

GLUTEN-FREE ◆

Making my drink
Peel the oranges and remove the seeds. Cut the carrots into pieces and peel the ginger. Put all the ingredients through a juicer.

Drink immediately.

GREEN
SMOOTHIE

MAKES 4 GLASSES
PREPARATION TIME: 5 MINUTES

INGREDIENTS
½ CUCUMBER, PEELED AND SEEDED
JUICE OF ½ LIME
⅔ CUP (5 FL OZ/150 ML) GRAPEFRUIT JUICE
(1 PINK GRAPEFRUIT)
1 AVOCADO
2 LARGE HANDFULS (1¾ OZ/50 G) ARUGULA
2 MINT SPRIGS, LEAVES PICKED
1 CUP (8 FL OZ/250 ML) COCONUT WATER
½ CUP (4 FL OZ/100 ML) WATER

GLUTEN-FREE ◆

Making my drink
Process all the ingredients together in a blender, or a food processor if you don't have a blender. Extend with a few ice cubes if necessary.

Drink immediately.

Indexes

MENU PLANS

RECIPE GUIDE

INDEX BY
INGREDIENT

4 WEEKS
OF MENU PLANS

Week
1
(Spring / Summer)

Monday Fast Day	Tuesday Non-Fast Day	Wednesday Non-Fast Day	Thursday Fast Day	Friday Non-Fast Day	Saturday Non-Fast Day	Sunday Non-Fast Day
	Breakfast	Breakfast		Breakfast	Breakfast	Brunch:
♦ Black rice, peas, asparagus & mint (p. 64)	♦ Thai tartare (p. 144) ♦ Black rice (p. 124) ♦ Steamed broccoli & soy sauce (p. 110)	♦ Pot luck salad with smoked mackerel (p. 170)	♦ Pasta salad (p. 78)	♦ Tuna dip & crudités (p. 114) ♦ Omelette with ham, tomato & salad (p. 140)	♦ Spicy chickpea salad (p. 162) ♦ Green salad with herbs (p. 111) ♦ Cheese	♦ Express juice! (p. 198) ♦ The club sandwich (p. 180)
	♦ Grilled chicken & crunchy salad (p. 194) ♦ Quinoa (p. 124)	♦ Beef carpaccio (p. 182) ♦ Crisp & tangy salad (p. 102)		♦ Miso soup revisited (p. 120) ♦ Fish tartare (p. 172) ♦ Red rice ♦ 2 glasses of wine	♦ Grilled fish & vegetable mash (p. 178) ♦ Dessert ♦ 2 glasses of wine	♦ Thai duck breast & cellophane noodles (p. 192) ♦ Dessert ♦ 2 glasses of wine

Week
2
(Spring / Summer)

Monday Fast Day	Tuesday Non-Fast Day	Wednesday Non-Fast Day	Thursday Fast Day	Friday Non-Fast Day	Saturday Non-Fast Day	Sunday Non-Fast Day
	Breakfast	Breakfast		Breakfast	Breakfast	Brunch:
♦ Quinoa, tomatoes, preserved lemon & fresh herbs (p. 38)	♦ Salmon chirashi revisited (p. 174)	♦ Spring asparagus (p. 104) ♦ Tomato tart (p. 100)	♦ Al dente vegetables & eggs (p. 36)	♦ Chicken brochettes with lemongrass (p. 142) ♦ Grilled green beans (p. 113)	♦ Asparagus, zucchini & feta salad (p. 161) ♦ Super tabbouleh (p. 163)	♦ Green smoothie (p. 198) ♦ Omelette with ham, tomato & salad (p. 140)
	♦ Steamed fish & crisp green beans (p. 130)	♦ Fennel & endive salad (p. 158) ♦ Beef meatballs (p. 143)		♦ Creamy gazpacho (p. 152) ♦ Zucchini & shrimp (p. 132) ♦ 2 glasses of wine	♦ Nice & spicy beef salad (p. 145) ♦ Black rice (p. 124) ♦ Dessert ♦ 2 glasses of wine	♦ Thai-style pork (p. 188) ♦ Dessert ♦ 2 glasses of wine